Wellington
Shropshire
The Road to Revival

Wellington
Shropshire
The Road to Revival

By Dr Tadzio Jodlowski

Souvenir Edition

Published by Kabelmaxer
© Tadzio Jodlowski 2024
First Edition

The right of Tadzio Jodlowski to be identified as the author of this work has been asserted by him in accordance with the Copyright Designs and Patents Act of 1988.

All rights reserved. No part of this publication may be reproduced, distributed, or transmitted in any form or by any means, including photocopying, recording, or other electronic or mechanical methods, without the prior written permission of the publisher, except in the case of brief quotations embodied in critical reviews and certain other non-commercial uses permitted by copyright law.

For permission requests, write to the publisher at the following address, addressed "Attention: Permissions Coordinator." Inquiries should be addressed via email to the following address: rescuer. Tv

"A market town is more than just a place to buy and sell; it's a gathering point for the dreams and aspirations of its inhabitants."

Anon

"Returning to Shropshire, I was impressed by a sense of revival in my hometown created by Wellington town council's regeneration partnership, "Love Wellington," and a group of dedicated business owners. Inspired by this endeavour, I decided to capture their stories and give them a well-deserved round of applause".

This is our Wellington Magazine: May 2024

Table of Contents

About the Author ix

Dedication xi

Foreword by Mandy Thorn MBE DL xiii

Cordial wishes from the Wellington History Group xv

Acknowledgements xvii

Preface xix

Part One: Inspiring thoughts on the revival of Wellington, Shropshire 1

    Introduction 3

    Chapter 1: Farewell to Cladchester 5

    Chapter 2: Good Morning Squire... how's your Shire? 11

    Chapter 3: The Scrobbesbyrigscr Lad 19

    Chapter 4: Thrice around the Wrekin 27

    Chapter 5: Respect the Countryside 35

    Chapter 6: Welcome to Wellingtonia 43

    Chapter 7: The Masurian Connection 51

    Chapter 8: Saturday Morning Rituals 59

    Chapter 9: The Doughnut Effect 69

    Chapter 10: The Edge of Chaos 77

    Chapter 11: The Revival Begins 85

    Chapter 12: Electric Wellington 93

    Chapter 13: International Wellington 101

    Chapter 14: Four hours to save Wellington! 111

    Chapter 15: Conclusion 117

Part Two: Interviews with business owners and those involved with Wellington's revival 125

    Chapter 1: Sally Themans Director 127

    Chapter 2: Paola Armstrong Administrator 139

    Chapter 3: The Wellington Cobbler 149

    Chapter 4: Mark's Barbers 157

    Chapter 5: The Gaming Café 163

    Chapter 6: The Guitar Vault 173

    Chapter 7: Leslie's Larder 181

    Chapter 8: Gratitude Café 187

    Chapter 9: Spinning Records 199

    Chapter 10: The Little Pantry 209

    Chapter 11: Wrekin Framers 215

    Chapter 12: The Orbit Cinema 223

    Chapter 13: Wellington Angling 235

    Chapter 14: Wellington Cycle Delivery 239

    Chapter 15: The Pheasant Pub 251

    Chapter 16: Wellington H2A 259

    Chapter 17: Anthony's of Wellington 277

Gallery 293

About the Author

Dr Tadzio Jodlowski is a lecturer, composer, and author with a lifelong interest in philosophy, psychology, and history. Throughout his career, he has made significant contributions to academia and the arts, inspiring numerous individuals with his insightful teachings and creative works.

He has worked at renowned institutions such as BBC North and the Manchester Metropolitan University Business School. His most recent role is as an esteemed faculty member at the University of Staffordshire, where he has been instrumental in guiding and mentoring students, imparting his knowledge and expertise to the next generation of professionals in the field.

This is Dr Jodlowski's third book. His first, "How to Manage Rescuer Feelings in a Post-Pandemic World," explores the psychological effects of the pandemic on the younger generation, offering guidance and understanding. His second book, "The Great Prince Harry Mystery," presents a captivating narrative about a rescuer prince, blending historical intrigue with psychological depth.

Dr Jodlowski's unique blend of expertise and creativity makes his works enlightening and engaging, cementing his place as a respected voice in his areas of interest. He is currently working on his fourth book and plans to present readers with groundbreaking and original publications on a variety of subjects.

Dedication

This book is dedicated to the memory of Stasia Byk, who worked in the town and always loved Wellington.

Foreword by Mandy Thorn MBE DL

The role of the modern High Sheriff is to keep the King's Peace, support the judiciary and those charged with upholding law and order, to thank the wider emergency services, charities and community groups within our county, and to shine a spotlight on our towns and villages. High Sheriffs serve for one year in a completely voluntary capacity with no recourse to public funds and have the extraordinary privilege of being able to meet so many citizens of their county and see the incredible work that goes on each and every day.

Shropshire is a special place, the largest inland county in England, and unusual in not having a city at its centre. It does however have 22 towns within its ceremonial county boundary, 18 of which are recognised as market towns. Wellington, within the administrative area of the Borough of Telford and Wrekin, is one of the larger towns within the county.

As High Sheriff of Shropshire in 2023-24 I had the privilege of visiting Wellington as a guest of the Town Council as part of their "Love Wellington" campaign as well as spending time in the town with the amazing Street Pastors on one of their evening patrols. Wellington has seen many changes over the last 1000 years; from the Norman Conquest to the Industrial Revolution to the creation of the New Town of Telford. Wellington has always had a part to play in the history of Shropshire and so it is only fitting that this book will inform us all about this fascinating town.

Cordial wishes from the Wellington History Group

Standing still gets us nowhere. This is particularly true of communities.

Looking back at Wellington's history there have been many times when individuals or groups of people have made changes that have taken the town forward. In 1854, an Improvements Committee was set up. Its job was to maintain standards and invest in new ideas, such as gas lamps that made the streets both brighter and safer.

Wellington was at the forefront when it provided a well-baby clinic, cookery classes in school to improve eating standards, and council housing, to mention just a few local initiatives.

Individuals gave the town its first library, our prize-winning park and the now-lost cottage hospital. This book looks at our town in more recent times and follows the current steps being taken to keep up with and even lead the way, keeping the heart of our town beating.

Let us move forward together and celebrate Wellington under the Wrekin.

Wellington History Group

Illustrations created by the author using AI.

Acknowledgements

I would like to express my gratitude to all those who consented to be interviewed for this book and those who provided additional material. I would also like to thank Mrs. Irena Jodlowski for sharing her memories of Wellington and contributing to my research.

Preface

As I sit down to pen these words, I am filled with gratitude for the countless individuals who have made this endeavour possible. This book on the revival of Wellington, Shropshire, is not solely my creation; it is the culmination of the collective wisdom, memories, and experiences generously shared by the community members who call this vibrant town their home.

I extend my deepest appreciation to all those who granted me interviews, shared anecdotes, and offered invaluable insights into Wellington's rich history and promising future. Your voices, woven into the fabric of these pages, illuminate the spirit and resilience of a community bound by shared aspirations and a commitment to progress.

In sharing these pages with you, I hope this book serves as a tribute to the resilience, ingenuity, and unwavering spirit of the Wellington community. May it stand as a testament to the power of collaboration and the enduring legacy of those who shape the places we call home.

Completing this book has been an interesting journey and one that unexpectedly touched me on a profound level. As I delved into the story of Wellington's revival, I found myself drawn into a narrative that mirrored the revival of my own life.

Documenting Wellington's revival, I discovered parallels with my personal journey of growth, renewal, and self-discovery.

I hope you will look upon this book not just as a souvenir but as a celebration of a specific moment in time when a highly motivated group of people came together and made positive change happen. It is a testament to their collective efforts, shared determination, and unwavering belief in a much-loved market town.

With thanks,

Dr Tadzio Jodlowski

Shropshire,

England.

Part One
Inspiring thoughts on the revival of Wellington, Shropshire

Introduction

Welcome to the journey of rediscovery, resilience, and revival that unfolds within the pages of this book. Here, we embark on a captivating exploration of Wellington, Shropshire, a town whose story transcends the boundaries of geography to touch the depths of the human spirit.

In the following chapters, we delve into the heart of Wellington's revival, tracing its evolution from a community facing challenges to one embracing opportunities for growth and transformation. Through a tapestry of narratives, anecdotes, and historical insights, we witness this town's remarkable journey - a journey that unexpectedly mirrors the revival of countless individual lives, including my own.

As we navigate through the highs and lows of Wellington's revitalization, we encounter tales of resilience, innovation, and collective action. We uncover the stories of ordinary individuals who, through their extraordinary efforts, became catalysts for change, breathing new life into the fabric of their community.

But this is more than just a story of a town's resurgence; it is a vivid reflection of the human experience - the universal quest for renewal, purpose, and belonging. Through the lens of Wellington's revival, we explore themes of unwavering perseverance, remarkable adaptability, and the enduring power of hope.

As we embark on this journey together, I invite you to play an active role in immersing yourself in the rich tapestry of experiences that define Wellington's revival. May this exploration serve as a source of inspiration, insight, and reflection - a testament to the indomitable spirit of communities and individuals alike.

So, let us turn the page and begin this odyssey of rediscovery - a journey that illuminates not only Wellington's path but also the boundless potential that resides within each of us. Welcome to the story of Wellington's revival - a story that resonates with the echoes of our own lives and the promise of a brighter tomorrow.

The book is structured into three parts. The first part contains my personal reflections and thoughts on Wellington. The second consists of interviews with business owners and organizers, and the third is a gallery of images which show revival in action.

Chapter One

Farewell to Cladchester

I have been living in Manchester for several years and working as a lecturer at the new MMUBS building on Oxford Road. Living in this city has been an amazing experience, with each day bringing unexpected encounters and a sense of adventure. I have explored the city and its various attractions, including art galleries and theatres. I have seen Leonardo Da Vinci's drawings at the Walker Gallery and the futuristic designs of Cesare Colombo. I have watched Gabrielle Drake at the Royal Exchange, Kate O'Mara at the Opera House, and Roger Moore at the Palace Theatre. Before working at MMUBS, I worked at BBC North, where I had the opportunity to meet Andrea Bocelli, Michael Apted, and the Corrs. I have interviewed scientists at Jodrell Bank and worked on the National Lottery. When city life gets too much, I escape in my car, driving down old country roads to familiar places I have known all my life.

My apartment in Manchester is on the second floor and has a balcony, I can see hills in the distance that remind me of Shropshire. Today is my last day at work and the last time I will teach my students. I enjoy hosting online sessions in my warm and cosy kitchen. However, my combi-heater has stopped working this morning, and it's cold. I teach students from around the country and try to make them realize that everyone is clever in different ways. I also manage the International Unit, which supports students from France, Germany, Italy, Spain, Poland, and Brazil. As I prepare for my lesson, a strong smell of exotic cigarettes begins to emerge from under the kitchen sink. The pipes in these apartments are interconnected, and ever since the Portuguese tenants moved in, there have been unusual odours in my kitchen. It all started when they received a large parcel from Amazon, and a plastic greenhouse appeared on their balcony. There is now a pungent smell in my kitchen each morning and late at night. It appears that someone is either making preparations for large-scale production or seeking a natural remedy for their rheumatism.

During today's online lesson with my students using *Microsoft Teams*, the atmosphere is lively and full of unexpected moments. Most of the students turn on their cameras and share greetings, but one student remains hidden, munching on his breakfast cereal while I begin the lesson. To lighten the mood, I share a humorous anecdote about Kellogg's "Crave" cereal and its unique marketing strategy, using the word "munchies" to create a comical mental image tied to *Geodemographic* Theory. The discussion sparks an engaging conversation about how this theory is applied in business to identify potential customers. It is fascinating to analyse how this marketing campaign fell short because it was launched when the students were away for Easter. As the two-hour session comes to an end, we bid each other farewell. I decided to leave quietly without telling them that this is my last lesson. The students leave cheerful comments and symbols in the chat section, bringing our time together to a joyful end. Their final messages mean a lot to me:

Bye Tadzio 😊

Thank you Tadzio 👨‍🏫

Great lesson, as always... 🎯

Have a nice break! 🌄

I spend time browsing the internet to distract myself and keep up with what's happening in the world. It's good news - it seems that we have entered the *endemic* phase of a global pandemic and can start to lead normal lives again. It feels like only yesterday when I watched a livestream tracking the emergence of this awful virus. Thank goodness it's over, and we can get out and about again, breathe fresh air, and spend time with our loved ones. Lately, I've been thinking about returning to the peaceful embrace of the countryside. However, I have noticed some pieces of wood that are part of my balcony, and they are about to cause me a great deal of trouble. I contact an estate agent in Didsbury, and my apartment soon appears on their website. However, when a chartered surveyor arrives one morning, he has a worried look on his face and keeps a low profile. When he sends me his report a week later, it contains a shocking revelation - those innocent pieces of wood are identified as 10% cladding! This is a significant issue that will affect anyone in the city who wants to sell their property...and so, a long and troubling ordeal begins for me and many others. Over the next few months, a procession of potential buyers crosses the threshold, but their initial enthusiasm is always tempered by emerging stories about cladding. In order to sell my apartment, I must obtain a certificate, but no one wants to issue one. The government states that you don't need a certificate for a property that is six stories high, but the building societies do not agree!

Hundreds of apartments are now trapped in a cladding nightmare and cannot be sold. The cladding on numerous apartment buildings has plunged their owners into a distressing and uncertain situation. This has created a complex mix of financial instability and emotional turmoil that is being experienced by many. These homeowners are now living in a state of anxiety, desperately trying to sell their properties while coming to terms with a new reality. Their most valuable asset has been tarnished by a problem beyond their control, leaving them feeling powerless and exposed. The ongoing uncertainty serves as a constant reminder of their predicament, overshadowing what was once a place of security. As they come to grips with their circumstances, the homeowners face the formidable challenge of traversing legal, financial, and emotional obstacles.

Life in the city and the countryside offers incredibly unique and exhilarating experiences. The city pulsates with non-stop energy, teeming with diverse crowds navigating bustling streets and towering skyscrapers adorned with glittering lights. The atmosphere is electric, fuelled by a myriad of events and the lively symphony of car horns, sirens, and animated conversations. The air is filled with the tantalizing aroma of street food, the rich scent of coffee from corner cafes, and the intriguing hint of exhaust fumes. On the other hand, the countryside provides a serene escape, with expansive green landscapes stretching into the distance, dotted with charming rustic homes. The tranquil sounds of chirping birds, rustling leaves, and the gentle flow of nearby streams create a harmonious contrast. The air is infused with the refreshing fragrance of grass, wildflowers, and the earthy aftermath of rain showers.

The city is a vibrant, bustling metropolis that is always full of energy and excitement. At night, the streets light up with neon signs and the movement of people. The city transforms into a dreamscape at night, and couples walk through Chinatown, and the red paper lanterns sway in the breeze. In contrast, the countryside at night becomes a tranquil oasis, a haven of peace and quiet. The unpolluted sky becomes a canvas of twinkling stars, a rare sight in urban areas. The symphony of nature, with its distant nocturnal sounds and gentle whispers of the wind, creates a serene ambience. Disconnecting from modern technology, the countryside invites you to fully embrace the tranquillity of the night. The crisp air carries the refreshing scents of pine and grass, providing a soothing respite for relaxation, reflection, and connection with the natural world.

As offers on my apartment dwindle and negotiations falter, I begin to lose hope of ever returning to the countryside. At the last minute, my estate agent receives a call from someone living in the block beside me. It turns out that she has a son who works in Dubai, and they want to increase their portfolio. Her favourite band is Led Zeppelin…she is obviously a person of good character! It's a great result, and she agrees to buy my property. It's time to say farewell to Cladchester and see what's going on in good old Shropshire!

Chapter Two

Good Morning Squire... how's your Shire?

The Anglo-Saxons established a governance system based on 'shires' in England, which were regions for efficient administration. However, the Norman invasion of 1066 changed the cultural and linguistic landscape of the country, and the Normans introduced the term 'county', derived from the French' comté' to indicate these divisions. This combination of Anglo-Saxon legacy with Norman innovation represents a significant moment in history that still influences the region today. England has 48 ceremonial counties, each with its own unique character and a rich, storied history. These places, often seen as just bureaucratic lines on an old map, have a depth of history that commands respect and appreciation. The more you explore them, the more you uncover. Each county has a story to tell, from Cornwall's rugged coastline to Yorkshire's green hills. Whether they're called counties or shires, these places hold a special place in the hearts of the people who live there. A little research can reveal a treasure trove of historical significance about the shire you live in and provide you with a renewed interest in your local town.

England is home to many shires, from the well-known Lancashire, Lincolnshire, and Hampshire to the lesser-known Kinross-shire in Scotland. Shropshire, for example, covers an area of 1,343 square miles and has a population of around 441,498. It is known for its rural and sparsely populated nature and its rich geological history. This includes more rocks of different ages than any area of comparable size in the world. The largest and most well-known rock formation is the volcanic rock that forms the local landmark called the Wrekin. Archaeological evidence suggests that the area has been inhabited since prehistoric times, with ancient hill forts and burial mounds scattered throughout the landscape. The remnants of early settlements are a reminder of the countless generations that have occupied this land.

Throughout the centuries, Shropshire has been shaped by various invaders, including the Romans, Saxons, and Normans, each leaving their mark on the region's culture and heritage. From the high basilica wall at Wroxeter to the Norman castles that dot the countryside, the layers of history in Shropshire remain accessible and provide visitors with a glimpse of the past. It is the largest landlocked shire in England and remains mostly rural, with some areas of industrialization. There are places like Ruyton-XI-Towns that represent a merger of multiple townships, as well as many scenic villages waiting to be discovered while exploring its backroads with unusual names such as Ditton Priors, Stottesdon, and Little Ness.

There are said to be six main towns in Shropshire:

Shrewsbury: Known for its medieval streets and historical architecture, known as one of the main towns in Shropshire, offering a mix of history and tradition

Ludlow: A picturesque town with a rich history, famous for its beautiful landscapes, historic buildings, and numerous festivals

Ironbridge: Renowned for being the birthplace of the world's first iron bridge, with its living museum at Blist's Hill providing a glimpse of its proud industrial past

Bridgnorth: A town with a unique funicular mode of transport, providing stunning views, a popular heritage railway, and classic car restoration

Whitchurch: Known for its quaint charm and historic significance, as well as being the place where a popular auction house resides.

Much Wenlock: Featuring a wealth of historic architecture, including timber-framed buildings, medieval streets, and the picturesque ruins of Wenlock Priory, dating back to the 12th century.

However, I would suggest that there is another one that is worthy of investigation, and that is a town called:

Wellington: This town received a royal market charter in 1244 and hosted the first Shropshire Olympian Games in 1861. It is located 3 miles from The Wrekin, which offers panoramic views of 17 counties.

The towns and villages of Shropshire are a testament to its rich cultural history. From the bustling market towns of Shrewsbury and Oswestry to the quaint hamlets surrounded by rolling hills, each has its own unique charm and character. In Ludlow, the streets are lined with timber-framed buildings, while Bridgnorth's cliff railway provides scenic views of the surrounding countryside. Additionally, the picturesque villages of Much Wenlock and Church Stretton offer a glimpse into traditional rural life with their thatched cottages and thriving community spirit. Combined with the county's stunning natural scenery, Shropshire's towns and villages create a captivating tapestry of past and present, where history meets modernity amidst a backdrop of timeless beauty.

Growing up in Shropshire offers an opportunity to experience a pace of life that is timeless and charming, with green fields stretching as far as the eye can see and life remaining unchanged in many ways. Here, the tranquil rhythm of life invites you to savour each moment amidst the peaceful countryside. Shropshire has a wealth of good food and drink establishments, with culinary delights crafted from locally sourced ingredients. From hearty farm-fresh meals to quaint country pubs serving up ales brewed with artisanal care, every bite and sip is a celebration of tradition and flavour. Nature reigns supreme in Shropshire, with sprawling woodlands, meandering rivers, and majestic hills waiting to be explored. Whether wandering through ancient forests or hiking along scenic trails, the beauty of the natural world envelops visitors in a sense of wonder and awe.

Despite its rural and timeless appeal, Shropshire is also home to many creative businesses and entrepreneurial projects. These represent a mixture of history and tradition and some new developments we shall visit later in this book. The region has shown a sense of innovation and creativity, which has been an important part of its recovery from recent events. As the world emerges from the shadows of the pandemic, Shropshire presents post-pandemic opportunities to anyone who wishes to reconnect with loved ones and embrace the joys of community once more. Under such circumstances gatherings with friends and family take on new meaning as cherished moments to celebrate the simple pleasures of togetherness.

In Shropshire, the road ahead is one of hope and resilience, where the promise of brighter days beckons. As we navigate the path back to normalcy, Shropshire stands as a timeless sanctuary, offering solace, rejuvenation, and the comforting embrace of home. The pandemic has underscored the value of fresh air and open spaces, and now, more than ever, people are flocking to the countryside to savour these simple pleasures. Strolling through Shropshire's picturesque villages, families and friends gather outdoors, enjoying picnics in verdant meadows and walks along the tranquil River Severn. The renewed appreciation for nature's beauty is palpable, with residents and visitors alike taking time to marvel at the rolling hills, ancient woodlands, and vibrant wildlife. Everywhere in the countryside, life is blossoming anew. Local markets are bustling once more, with vendors offering fresh produce, homemade crafts, and friendly conversation. Village greens echo with the laughter of children and the sounds of community events resuming after a long hiatus. Country pubs and tea rooms are filled with patrons savouring hearty meals and the joy of shared company.

This revival is a testament to the enduring spirit of rural communities, resilient and optimistic in the face of adversity. Yet, we have only begun to understand the profound impact of the intense introspection brought about by the pandemic. Many have emerged from this period with a changed outlook, valuing simplicity, connection, and the natural world more deeply than before. The experience of prolonged isolation and the subsequent return to community life has prompted a re-evaluation of priorities. People are now more attuned to the importance of mental well-being, the benefits of slowing down, and the joy found in everyday moments. This shift in perspective has infused the countryside with a renewed sense of purpose. Residents and newcomers alike are keen to preserve the serenity and charm of rural life, fostering a deeper respect for the environment and each other. The sense of community in Shropshire is stronger than ever, with neighbours looking out for one another, sharing in local events, and supporting small businesses. Respect for the place and its people remains paramount, ensuring that Shropshire continues to be a haven of peace and rejuvenation for all who call it home or respectfully visit it.

Chapter Three

The Scrobbesbyrigscr Lad

The most famous collection of poems about this county is undoubtedly "The Shropshire Lad" by A.E. Housman, written in 1896. The question I will ask here is, have you read it? I have, and it merits its status as a timeless classic. It's due to lines like this that discuss naivety:

> *"When I was one-and-twenty*
> *I heard a wise man say,*
> *'Give crowns and pounds and guineas*
> *But not your heart away;*
> *Give pearls away and rubies*
> *But keep your fancy free.'*
> *But I was one-and-twenty,*
> *No use to talk to me."*

These lines encourage the reader to shift between celebratory and melancholic moods:

> *"The time you won your town the race*
> *We chaired you through the market-place;*
> *Man and boy stood cheering by,*
> *And home we brought you shoulder-high.*
> *Today, the road all runners come,*
> *Shoulder-high we bring you home,*
> *And set you at your threshold down,*
> *Townsman of a stiller town."*

A.E. Housman's connection to Shropshire stems from his family roots and upbringing rather than a specific event. However, he did spend some time at his family home in Fockbury, located in the neighbouring county of Worcestershire. When embarking on a creative project, it is important to choose a title early to stimulate your imagination. A.E. Housman had to choose between using "Shropshire" or "Scrobbesbyrigscr" in his title, and you can see why he chose the shorter version. The longer word means "the shire of the scrubland hill fort." With apologies to A.E. Housman, I have written a poem using the longer word and called it "The Scrobbesbyrigscr Lad".

The Scrobbesbyrigscīr Lad
(In the style of A.E. Housman)

In Scrobbesbyrigscīr's ancient fold,
Where tales of love are sweetly told,
There dwells a lad with heart so true,
His love a beacon, bright and new.

Upon the moor, where he doth roam,
His eyes alight with love's own dome,
He dreams of her, his tender maid,
In Scrobbesbyrigscīr's silent glade.

Beneath the stars, their whispers weave,
A dance of hearts that never leave,
For in his soul, her name does stir,
The maiden of Scrobbesbyrigscīr.

Through fields of gold and meadows fair,
He seeks her love beyond compare,
With every step, his passion flies.

In twilight's hue, his heart does yearn,
For her, whose love he seeks to earn.
Amidst the dusk, his hope alights.

Beneath the boughs of ancient trees,
He whispers vows upon the breeze.
In nature's embrace, his love takes flight.

Let us explore the fascinating world of A.E. Housman in more detail! A literary genius whose influence goes beyond his renowned work, "The Shropshire Lad." In his second volume of poetry, "Last Poems," he explores themes of loss, unrequited love, and the passage of time with unparalleled emotional depth. But that's not all - "More Poems," released posthumously, offers a treasure trove of previously unpublished verses that continue to resonate with his emotive style. Housman wasn't just a poet but also a revered classical scholar renowned for his meticulous work on the textual criticism of Latin poetry. His lectures and academic writings reveal his influential role in the field of classical studies. Housman was a figure of considerable renown among his contemporaries, admired for his poetry and classical scholarship.

Among poets, Housman's work was recognized for its lyrical simplicity and emotional depth. Poet and critic Edmund Blunden praised "A Shropshire Lad" for its "classic" nature, emphasizing its "freshness and delicacy" and its ability to capture universal themes in an accessible manner. Housman's colleagues in classical scholarship held him in high esteem for his rigorous and meticulous approach to textual criticism. Fellow classicist and scholar J.P. Postgate acknowledged Housman's formidable expertise, referring to him as a "man of remarkable acumen and learning." However, Housman's personality also drew notable comments from his peers. Known for his reserved and often aloof demeanour, novelist and critic Virginia Woolf described him as a "cold and solitary figure," yet she also recognized the deep emotional undercurrents in his poetry that resonated with readers. Housman's sometimes acerbic wit and critical nature were also well-documented, adding to the enigmatic aura that surrounded him. A.E. Housman's contemporaries saw him as a complex figure: a poet of exquisite melancholy and simplicity, a scholar of remarkable precision and rigour, and a person whose reserved exterior belied his work's profound emotional and intellectual depths. Their varied reflections paint a picture of a highly respected and somewhat enigmatic man, leaving a lasting impact on both literature and classical studies.

"Scrobbesbyrigscr Lad" is an Old English term specifically referring to a young man from Shrewsbury. In contrast "Shropshire Lad" is a modern term that can refer to any young man from Shropshire, with additional literary significance due to A.E. Housman's poetry. The historical and cultural ties between Shrewsbury and Wellington are nothing short of thrilling. These two towns in Shropshire have an incredibly rich and intertwined history that brings together their unique stories into a shared narrative of the county. Shrewsbury, originally known as "Scrobbesbyrig" in Saxon times, has been a central hub of political, economic, and cultural activity since medieval times. Its strategic location along the River Severn made it a pivotal point for trade and governance. Just 12 miles to the east, Wellington has been a bustling market town since medieval times. Nestled at the foot of Wrekin Hill, it has long been a centre for agricultural trade, with its market charter dating back to the 13th century. The town's historical significance is further highlighted by its role in the Industrial Revolution, playing a crucial part in the coal and iron industries.

The connection between Shrewsbury and Wellington is truly multifaceted and thrilling:

Economic Ties: The two towns were integral parts of Shropshire's economy, with Wellington's market complementing Shrewsbury's bustling trading hub. Merchants and traders routinely travelled between the two towns, fostering a strong economic bond.

Transport and Communication: The construction of canals and railways in the 18th and 19th centuries further strengthened the link between Shrewsbury and Wellington, enhancing commercial and social interactions.

Cultural Exchange: Festivals, fairs, and markets in Shrewsbury and Wellington attracted visitors from both towns, blending cultural practices, traditions, and dialects, creating a shared Shropshire identity.

Historical Events: Both towns have witnessed and contributed to significant historical events, including the English Civil War, which saw Shrewsbury as a royalist stronghold and Wellington as a site of skirmishes and troop movements.

Educational and Social Links: Educational institutions like Shrewsbury School drew students from across Shropshire, including Wellington. Notable families often had estates and interests spanning both towns.

The link between Shrewsbury and Wellington is emblematic of Shropshire's broader historical narrative– story of interconnected communities, economic interdependence, and shared cultural heritage. This bond is a testament to the enduring connections that define the county's past and present.

Regional poetry is a vibrant and essential part of the literary world, giving voice to specific locales' unique essence, culture, and experiences. Regional poets provide a rich, textured understanding of their surroundings through vivid imagery, local dialects, and intimate depictions. This not only preserves a region's cultural and historical identity but also allows readers to gain insight into and appreciation for places they may never visit. Regional poetry enriches the literary landscape by diversifying the range of human experiences and perspectives, ensuring that the voices and stories of all areas are heard and valued. It fosters a greater sense of connection and empathy among disparate communities while celebrating the particularities that make each region unique. Additionally, regional poetry highlights local struggles, triumphs, and traditions, providing a platform for marginalized voices and lesser-known narratives. In this way, regional poetry enhances our literary heritage and contributes to a more inclusive and comprehensive understanding of the world.

The following examples illuminate how various literary works capture the beauty and essence of different rural regions in England. From William Wordsworth's enchanting poetry celebrating the natural splendour of the Lake District to Laurie Lee's evocative portrayal of rural life in the Cotswolds, Gloucestershire, each piece immerses readers in the idyllic charm of the English countryside. John Clare's rich verses depicting the rural landscapes of Northamptonshire and Thomas Hardy's poignant reflections on Dorset in "Wessex Poems and Other Verses" further transport us to these timeless locales. Ted Hughes's intense portrayal of the rugged Yorkshire landscape in "Remains of Elmet". Wellington's well-known poet, Philip Larkin's vivid snapshot of Northumberland's rural traditions in "Show Saturday" adds layers of depth and excitement to this exploration of literary tributes to England's countryside. All of these examples encourage readers to embark on a thrilling journey through the captivating and evocative landscapes of rural England.

Chapter Four

Thrice around the Wrekin

Nature operates as a continuous cycle of decline and revival. The countryside illustrates this perpetual dance, where the fall of ancient trees leads to new growth, and the remnants of past seasons nourish the earth for future blooms. While wildfires may scorch the land, they also create opportunities for fresh vegetation to thrive. This dynamic process of decay and regeneration showcases nature's resilience and adaptability. Understanding this cycle deepens our respect for the natural world and reminds us of the enduring promise of renewal, even after the harshest of times. In Shropshire, this ever-present cycle of life and rebirth mirrors our own journey, offering hope and the assurance that brighter days always lie ahead. There is a saying in Shropshire that when you procrastinate unnecessarily, you go "twice around the Wrekin". However, these days, with so many levels of complexity to deal with, we usually have to go *three times* around the Wrekin before anything gets done! The Wrekin, a remarkable hill, is adorned with several intriguing facets. Legend has it that a giant known as Gwendol Wrekin ap Shenkin ap Mynyddmawr, harbouring a grudge against the town of Shrewsbury, decided to flood the town and cause chaos for its inhabitants. He collected a large amount of earth and headed towards the town. While in the vicinity of a town called Wellington, he encountered a cobbler who was returning from Shrewsbury market with a large sack of worn shoes. The giant asked him for directions, stating that he was going to deposit his earth in the River Severn and flood the area. "It's a very long journey to Shrewsbury," the cobbler is said to have answered. "Look at all the shoes I've worn out walking from there! "The giant then abandoned his enterprise and deposited the earth on the ground beside him, where it became the Wrekin. The giant also removed the mud from his boots, which became the smaller hill called The Ercall, which stands next to it. The historic presence of the Wrekin has, therefore, given rise to a saying that is used to describe procrastination, and we can get philosophical about that.

The Wrekin, a geological marvel, is a rare sight-an eccentric formation known as a *faulted anticline*. This extraordinary structure is a result of powerful tectonic forces that fold rocks upwards, bestowing the hill with its unique shape and prominence in the landscape. At its peak, a mysterious mound, the "Wrekin Giant's Chair" or "Wrekin Rocking Stone", stands. This massive boulder, estimated to weigh around 137 tonnes, can be set in motion with some effort. The origin of the rock and its peculiar balancing act has aroused the interest of visitors for centuries. The Wrekin's geological peculiarity has not only captivated geologists but also sparked the imagination of many writers and poets over the years, including Mary Shelley, who was said to have been enthralled by the imposing silhouette of the Wrekin during her journeys to the region. However, the Wrekin's significance transcends its geological wonder. It has been a symbol of local folklore, artwork, and literature, embodying the region's rich cultural heritage and continues to do so.

The Wrekin is an extraordinary landmark that boasts geological, mythological, and cultural significance. It holds a treasure trove of stories and secrets that are waiting to be discovered by anyone visiting the county. The Wrekin can also be utilized as a symbol of endurance and motivation by drawing interesting theories from it. We can contemplate how it can take several attempts to achieve something and, in some cases, going round and round until an opportunity emerges. Motivation, much like the arduous journey of circumnavigating the Wrekin, requires a relentless drive and unwavering determination. Yet, it is the persistence to continue despite such difficulties that makes the adventure worthwhile. Going thrice around the Wrekin can be compared to a motivational theory rooted in the philosophy of perseverance and resilience. We can call this theory the Wrekin Persistence Theory (WPT). This theory suggests that success is rarely achieved through a one-time effort but rather through a relentless commitment to trying the same thing repeatedly until the desired outcome is attained. Central to the WPT is the recognition that setbacks and failures are inevitable parts of the journey toward success. Instead of viewing these setbacks as insurmountable obstacles, individuals following this theory can embrace them as valuable learning experiences that inform and refine their approach.

Key principles of Wrekin Persistence Theory:

Persistent Action: Success is the result of ongoing efforts and the ability to adapt based on feedback and outcomes. Through a process of continuous refinement, individuals are able to get closer to their goals, building upon previous efforts and accumulating knowledge and experience along the way.

Resilience in the Face of Failure: Rather than becoming discouraged by setbacks, individuals practising WPT maintain a resilient mindset, viewing failure as a natural part of the learning process. They use setbacks as opportunities for reflection and growth, identifying areas for improvement and adapting their strategies accordingly.

Incremental Progress: Success is seen as the result of incremental progress made through consistent effort over time. Each action brings individuals one step closer to their objective, gradually narrowing the gap between their current state and their desired outcome.

Goal Orientation: Individuals following WPT maintain a clear focus on their goals, using them as a guiding force to drive their actions and decisions. They break down larger objectives into smaller, manageable tasks, allowing them to maintain momentum and track their progress effectively.

Nighttime Beacon: WPT practitioners remember that there is a beacon at the top of the Wrekin that shines all night, even when we are asleep. Its presence inspires a sense of unconscious direction for those who are driven by purpose, even as they rest. In its luminance lies a testament to the power of determination, a beacon of hope that fuels dreams and aspirations.

Although "WPT" is a product of my imagination for entertainment purposes, it aligns with the studies of researchers and psychologists who have emphasized the significance of persistence, resilience, and learning in achieving success. These aspects are also reflected in the efforts of a market town called Wellington, located near the Wrekin. Amidst the rolling hills and picturesque landscapes, the narrative of trying again and again intertwines with the town's ongoing efforts to turn its fortunes around. Just as individuals persist in their endeavours despite setbacks, Wellington has faced several challenges, with each marking a new chapter in its journey towards revival. The transformation of Wellington into a pedestrian-friendly area symbolizes an initial attempt to breathe new life into the town, demonstrating the community's determination to adapt and evolve. Subsequent endeavours, such as the installation of "The Makers' Dozen Mural Trail", introduced a mixture of historical awareness and creativity to Wellington's landscape, showcasing the town's capacity for renewal and innovation.

The changes happening in Wellington, from the pedestrian-friendly initiatives to the introduction of Maker's Murals and the potential exhibited by the Orbit Cinema, reflect the town's ongoing journey of organic evolution. Each endeavour builds upon the last, pushing Wellington closer to its aspirations, much like circling the Wrekin. Progress often requires embracing change, navigating obstacles, and persisting in our efforts, even when the path seems daunting. The closure of the Clifton Cinema seemed unnecessary, and there were some heroic attempts to keep it open. In its place, there is a new view of the Wrekin, a new horizon - a testament to the resilience of Wellington's landscape and its inhabitants. The rise of out-of-town developments, exemplified by Telford Town Centre, posed formidable challenges to Wellington's traditional landscape and community fabric. Amidst the allure of convenience and modernity, the town remained resilient, clinging to its identity and sense of community. Telford Town Centre may have cast a shadow over Wellington, but it failed to extinguish the local pride and resilience that existed within its streets. In the face of these challenges, Wellington embarked on a journey of adaptation and reinvention, recognizing that survival hinged upon its ability to find creative solutions.

The community did not give in to despair but instead came together, embracing innovation and creativity to establish an independent identity in the evolving retail environment. Projects like pedestrian-friendly initiatives and the creation of Makers Murals were not just surface changes but strategic moves to revitalize Wellington's appeal and redefine its relevance in the modern era. Although Telford Town Centre initially drew attention away from Wellington, the town's resilience and determination ultimately became its greatest strength. As the appeal of malls diminished, people sought authenticity and connection, qualities embodied by Wellington's history and strong community spirit. In this changing landscape, Wellington emerged not as a victim of progress but as a symbol of resilience - a testament to the enduring power of community and the timeless appeal of authenticity in a world that is constantly changing. What is remarkable is that despite all the challenges it faced:

Wellington never died!

Time ebbs and flows, yet the Wrekin remains steadfast, standing tall as a sentinel of constancy amidst the shifting tides of life. Through the ages, it has been anchored in the landscape, serving as a testament to endurance and strength. The unwavering resolve of those who face the passage of time is embodied in the Wrekin's presence, which endures unyielding and timeless. Its steadfastness reminds us that while the world may change, some foundations remain unshaken, standing as beacons of stability in an ever-evolving world. Through the annals of history, epochs have risen and fallen, yet the silhouette of the Wrekin remains etched against the horizon, a steadfast monument to resilience. It stands as a silent witness to the passage of time, weathering the storms of centuries with unwavering poise. Like a guardian of memory, it holds the stories of generations within its rugged embrace, an enduring symbol of continuity amid the flux of existence. "Vivat Wellingtonia!"

Chapter Five

Respect the Countryside

It is early Sunday morning on the outskirts of Shrewsbury, and I am taking my dog for his first walk of the day. As we make our way, I come across a lush, green, open field covered in dew. The field is empty except for some mature trees and a group of docile cows in the distance. I'm not familiar with this field and ask a local who is walking past for his advice.

"Is it safe to walk across this field when there are cows in it?

The answer comes back:

"Yes, you can...I do it all the time!"

With newfound knowledge, I am ready to enjoy exploring this uncharted territory. My dog eagerly leads the way as we embark on an adventure through a vibrant landscape filled with new experiences. As we traverse the field, I am amazed by the dramatic impact of countless cow hooves, creating a rugged terrain. Amidst the journey, the melodious chirping of birds fills the air, complementing the endless blue sky above. It's a glorious morning in Shropshire, and I am invigorated by the challenge of navigating this dynamic environment. Full of exhilaration and freedom, I embrace this picturesque moment. But what unexpected excitement awaits around the next corner?

As I venture across the field with my faithful dog by my side, I spot a calm Friesian cow who appears to be the leader of the herd. My dog senses something amiss and lets out a protective bark, setting off a chain of events that is simultaneously comical and perilous. The once indifferent Friesian cow is now triggered, and her demeanour shifts from nonchalant to passive-aggressive. Despite the warning signs, I continue my walk with my dog, savouring the tranquillity of the surroundings. The Friesian cow seems distant at first, but there is a noticeable change in direction, and the rest of the herd is stirred as well. Suddenly, the Friesian starts moving in my direction, and the rest of the herd follows suit. My dog looks up at me, emitting a sound that conveys a sense of impending danger in canine language. He tries to protect me, but it's clear that he's no match for what's headed our way. I haven't touched beef for many years, but several tons of beef has now decided it is going to touch me! In this moment of uncertainty, I express my gratitude to my loyal dog and make a split-second decision. Recalling advice from a dog trainer, I release my dog so he can sprint to safety. He dashes towards the gate with remarkable speed. Meanwhile, I am faced with the daunting task of sprinting across a field of craters, my focus reaching an existential level. What started as a potentially dangerous encounter is now resembling a chaotic symphony as the herd voices its collective displeasure...a bovine rhapsody. Nevertheless, I am determined to emerge from this tragicomedy unscathed and live to face another day!

It has been suggested that in life, it's important to give the appearance of a serene swan gliding on the surface while you're paddling furiously. It's a delicate balance, like a high-stakes performance. I try to follow this advice, but due to my present circumstances, I end up looking like a worried swan doing a hundred miles an hour. Imagine facing a charging herd and trying to maintain an air of calm as you implement an orderly retreat. It's like becoming a martial artist, channelling focused meditation and observing the rhythm of the stampede. As the thundering hooves draw nearer, you must embody speed and efficiency, swiftly reaching the safety of the sidelines without stumbling or twisting an ankle. It feels as though the very earth is conspiring against you, with treacherous, sodden soil lying in wait to ensnare the unwary. To navigate this perilous terrain, you must balance yourself like a tightrope walker and make every effort not to fall. Every step requires utmost caution, as a single misjudgment could send you tumbling into the mire, unwittingly becoming part of nature's slapstick comedy. It's funny and it's serious at the same time!

I am pleased to report that I survived my close encounter with these cows, navigating through fields and narrowly avoiding a potential "cow-tastrophe! It's all part of the thrilling journey into the enchanting realm of country life, where every step is an exhilarating escapade. But townies, take care! Respecting the countryside and its ways is not just a matter of being polite; it's a fundamental principle of living in harmony with nature. The countryside is a sanctuary of life and natural beauty, with its vast fields, rolling hills, and peaceful meadows. It is a place where ecosystems thrive and wildlife flourishes, free from the noise and chaos of city life. To show respect for the countryside means to tread lightly on its earth, leaving only footprints and taking away memories. It means recognizing the rhythms of nature and understanding that every action has a ripple effect on the delicate balance of life. Whether it involves closing gates behind us, picking up litter, or staying on designated trails, every small gesture contributes to preserving the integrity of this precious landscape for future generations to enjoy. By treating the countryside with reverence and gratitude, we build a stronger connection to the land and its inhabitants, ensuring that its beauty and abundance continue to flourish.

The countryside is a collection of interconnected microsystems, each pulsing with life and energy. It's a place where the hard work of farmers and the wonders of nature converge in a grand orchestration. When we respect the countryside, we honour our place within this intricate balance and commit to preserving its beauty and vitality. Every rustling leaf and murmuring river holds ancient wisdom, speaking to the interconnectedness of all living things. Let's embrace the timeless ways of the countryside with humility and reverence, enriching our lives and securing its legacy for generations to come. In Shropshire, the road ahead is one of hope and resilience, where the promise of brighter days beckons. As we navigate the path back to normalcy, Shropshire stands as a timeless sanctuary, offering solace, rejuvenation, and the comforting embrace of home. The pandemic has underscored the value of fresh air and open spaces, and now, more than ever, people are flocking to the countryside to savour these simple pleasures. Strolling through Shropshire's picturesque villages, families and friends gather outdoors, enjoying picnics in verdant meadows and walks along the tranquil River Severn. The renewed appreciation for nature's beauty is palpable, with residents and visitors alike taking time to marvel at the rolling hills, ancient woodlands, and vibrant wildlife. As everywhere in the countryside springs back to life, it's important to remember that we share this space with a variety of animals, each with its own behaviours and rhythms. For instance, the cows that graze peacefully in Shropshire's fields are more than just picturesque elements of the landscape. They are sentient beings with distinct habits and social structures. Cows can be curious and gentle but can also become protective, especially when calves are present. Understanding and respecting their space is crucial. When walking through fields, it's wise to keep a safe distance, avoid sudden movements, and always close gates behind you to prevent disturbing their routines.

Following my dramatic walk across the field, I became fascinated by the concept of herd mentality. Cows are big, gentle creatures that are sometimes smarter than we realise. They are social butterflies - or should I say social cud-chewers who form strong bonds and show emotions such as fear and joy. They enjoy solving problems and are not as docile as they seem. Herd mentality in cows is like a bovine version of peer pressure. They stick together for safety and to find the best grazing spots. It's all about safety in numbers, which makes sense when you see things from their point of view. But don't think they can't think for themselves or that the don't have the capacity to think for themselves or act independently. I've seen cows break away from the group to explore a new patch of grass or decide they prefer a shady spot, even if their friends are soaking up the sun. It's like watching a cow say, "I hear you, but I'm doing my own thing". And let's not forget the cow hierarchy! It's important to remember that some cows act as leaders, some as followers, and then there are rebel cows who simply don't care about established rules.

So, when you're next to a pasture, take a moment to appreciate the cow drama unfolding. You'll see acts of leadership, moments of rebellion, and cows just being cows. They might be grazing in a group, but rest assured, each one has its own personality traits. Any newcomers embracing life in Shropshire need to understand and respect the behaviour of cows and wild animals in nature. This respect not only safeguards the well-being of the animals but also enriches their own experience, allowing them to fully appreciate the peace and rejuvenation that the countryside offers. By developing a deeper connection with nature and its creatures, everyone can contribute to the preservation of Shropshire's timeless beauty for generations to come.

Chapter Six

Welcome to Wellingtonia

Pour yourself a nice glass of wine, put on your headphones, play soothing Schubert string quartet music, and get ready to explore the independent state of *Wellingtonia*. As you traverse its streets and landmarks in your mind's eye, you will discover that this immersive experience is not just about learning facts; it's about delving into the soul of Wellington. Through this deep dive into its identity, you will enrich your knowledge of the town and awaken your anticipation for future visits, knowing that you will uncover new layers of its charm and character. In the realm of my imagination, *Wellingtonia* is an independent state where the past and present blend seamlessly, creating a timeless wonderland. In this place, each building tells a story of bygone eras while embracing the innovations of today. In *Wellingtonia*, the passage of time is not a linear journey but a fluid continuum, where the past is honoured, the present celebrated, and the future eagerly embraced. You can enter the state of Wellingtonia by purchasing a magazine of the same name at *Anthony's of Wellington*. This publication, a treasure trove of insights, is produced by *The Wellington History Group*, a dedicated group that has been active in the town since 2007, preserving its heritage and sharing its stories. I am currently immersed in their latest issue, number 35, and appreciate the seamless continuity that permeates years of dedicated research like a golden thread. This issue presents a variety of stories that capture the essence of Wellington's history and community spirit. From bidding farewell to the *Clifton Cinema*, a place filled with countless childhood memories, to reflecting on wartime experiences that still resonate with the town's older residents, each story is a powerful testament to the scale of Wellington's history. Tributes honouring local figures such as Miss Month, the bookseller, and Richard Hartshorne, the coalmaster, further enrich the narrative, offering a captivating glimpse into the town's past and present. Additionally, features on the Mallard Clock showcase the town's craftsmanship and heritage, while a touching tribute to Joyce Rogers celebrates her impact on Wellington's musical life. Through these engaging articles and profiles, the magazine provides a sense of connection and appreciation for the unique stories and characters that define Wellington's identity. As I delved into the work of this history group, I felt inspired to explore their archived issues online. Their first issue from 2007 is a testament to their dedication and passion for their craft. It reminds me that anything is possible with hard work and persistence, and this is a good opportunity to look at some of the back issues. The first issue of *Wellingtonia* introduces a group of local historians led by President George Evans and Chairman Allan Frost. They have compiled over thirty books about the town, and their dedication is echoed in the contributions of Joy Rebello and Phil Fairclough.

It is fascinating to learn that although the town received a charter for its market in 1244, an official town crest was not adopted until 1951. The first issue of *Wellingtonia* takes the reader back in time and showcases some of the town's buildings and mansions that have been demolished over the years. The publications capture how much has been lost over time. Issue 14 of 2013 has a blend of familiar local names and a few intriguingly exotic ones. For instance, Dave Weston's article on the individuals who performed at the *Clifton Cinema*, including The Great Nixon (the world's master mind reader) in 1939, offers a fascinating insight into the cinema's evolution over the years. Wendy Palin's attempt to identify the names on the Lych Gate illustrates the thoughtful nature of *Wellingtonia* and the people who produce it.

In the 24th issue, you can delve deeper into the history of the town. The issue covers a range of topics such as "Poets and Railways", which highlights the work of the first modern miserabilist, Philip Lakin, an article about microscopes, and *The Maker's Dozen Mural Trail*. The latter was developed by Rob Francis to attract more visitors to the town and painted by Paula Woof. The trail consists of twelve windows that showcase historical figures who created products in the town and modern makers and producers, such as the excellent Rowton Brewery. Primary research for *The Maker's Dozen Mural Trail* was carried out by Wellington H2A, which includes Rob and Anthony Nicholls and the Wellington History Group. The project reminds visitors of the town's rich history and encourages them to explore it further. *The Makers Dozen Mural Trail* represents an ingenious way to generate interest in Wellington while encouraging visitors to become regular visitors in the future.

The Wellington History Group and *Wellington H2A* have laid the groundwork for others to follow. A tangible example is the free magazine called *This is Our Wellington*. This serves as a platform for the aforementioned groups and others, providing a space for them to showcase their work and ideas. It also includes links to several groups and their websites, which provide a range of volunteer opportunities for anyone who is interested. Through these engaging articles and profiles, the magazine creates a sense of connection and appreciation for the unique stories and characters that define Wellington's identity. There are many valuable lessons that can be learned from historical groups in different parts of the world that have tried to revive their towns and cities. One such example is *The Bath Preservation Trust*, which was created by a group of conservationists and concerned citizens to protect the architectural heritage and character of Bath. Over the years, the Trust has become a leading advocate for preservation in the city, safeguarding Bath's architectural treasures and enhancing its reputation as a UNESCO World Heritage Site through restoration projects, conservation campaigns, and advocacy efforts.

The Trust is actively involved in various educational programs and outreach activities that engage the local residents, visitors, and school groups to raise awareness and appreciation of Bath's rich history and architecture. These initiatives include guided tours, workshops, lectures, and publications that provide insights into the city's architectural evolution and showcase archival collections containing valuable documents and photographs. The Trust aims to promote the importance of preserving and protecting the city's unique architectural and cultural heritage for future generations. Community engagement is at the core of the Trust's mission. It organizes events, exhibitions, and collaborative projects that celebrate Bath's architectural legacy and instil a sense of pride and ownership among residents. Moreover, the Trust is actively involved in advocacy work, including lobbying for heritage protection policies, responding to planning applications, raising awareness about threatened historic sites, and ensuring

Bath's architectural gems remain preserved for future generations. Looking ahead, the Trust remains committed to advancing historic preservation and education, relying on continued community support and collaboration to protect and celebrate Bath's cherished architectural heritage. From an international perspective, other historical groups are conducting similar work, such as ICOMOS, which works to protect and preserve historical places and sites worldwide. They are based in Paris, France and work closely with UNESCO to achieve their goals. ICOMOS provides guidance and advice to ensure that cultural heritage sites are protected and maintained for future generations. They do this by coordinating various activities such as research, training programs, and international cooperation.

Historical groups across the country and beyond are also working hard to preserve existing buildings and monuments. They go beyond simple preservation and strive to maintain historic sites' authenticity, integrity, and significance, ensuring that they remain accessible and meaningful to present and future communities. These groups play an important role in preserving their shared cultural heritage by advocating for sensitive development practices, offering educational programs, conducting research, and engaging with local communities. Through their advocacy for heritage protection policies, research, and community events, they work tirelessly to ensure that these irreplaceable assets are safeguarded against urban development or neglect. Historical groups preserve physical structures and uphold the stories, traditions, and memories embedded within them, enriching our understanding of the past and fostering a sense of continuity and connection across time and space.

In short, ICOMOS and historical groups work together to protect and preserve historical sites for future generations to cherish and learn from. *Wellingtonia* is always worth visiting - it's a place filled with interesting facts and historical landmarks that are well worth exploring. As you walk around the town's streets, you may notice a building that you have previously overlooked. However, now you can take a moment to appreciate its history and be pleasantly surprised to learn that some of the buildings in those photographs still exist! In my imagination, *Wellingtonia* is a place that merges Wellington's history with my own history and the history of any reader. In the independent state of *Wellingtonia*, everything resonates with the echoes of its past, inviting visitors to unravel its mysteries and forge their own connections to its history. Whether tracing the footsteps of ancestors who walked these streets centuries ago or simply marvelling at the timeless aspect of its surviving architecture, there's something enchanting about how *Wellingtonia* merges the past with the present, creating a tapestry of memories that transcends time. Preserving the history of one's town is a crucial task that pays tribute to the efforts of individuals, no matter how small they may seem, ensuring that their contributions are not lost with the passage of time. Every person has their own history book in the form of a family photo album; every town also has its own narrative waiting to be discovered. In these pages, we don't just see snapshots, but we glimpse the fabric of society, the customs, and the leadership that shaped the times. By documenting our town's history, we show respect to those who came before us, acknowledging their role in shaping the present and preserving their legacy for future generations.

Walking the streets of *Wellingtonia* takes on a whole new dimension when you are acquainted with its rich history and the stories of the people who have left their mark on its streets. With every step, the past comes alive, weaving a narrative that stretches back through the annals of time. The buildings are no longer just brick and mortar structures but living monuments to the dreams and aspirations of generations past. It's not just the grand landmarks that tell the tale of *Wellingtonia*'s history; the smaller, more intimate details also paint a vivid picture of daily life. The faded storefronts bear witness to the changing tides of commerce, while the ornate lampposts stand as silent sentinels, casting their warm glow upon the cobblestone pathways. As you pass by the town square, you can almost hear the echoes of bygone eras - the clatter of hooves on cobblestones, the chatter of market vendors, and the strains of music drifting through the air. Here, amidst the hustle and bustle of modern life, the past lingers like a cherished memory, waiting to be rediscovered by those who care to listen. Walking the streets of *Wellingtonia* with a deeper understanding of its history is not just a journey through time; it's a journey of the heart, where every corner holds a story waiting to be told. With each passing moment, you become a part of the tapestry of Wellingtonia's legacy, adding your own chapter to the vibrant tale of this storied town.

Chapter Seven

The Masurian Connection

There is a serene expanse of northeastern Poland that is known as the captivating land of Masuria. This mesmerising realm of lakes and legends has a way of captivating the soul like a siren's song. The tranquil waters and verdant forests create an environment where time appears to slow down, allowing one to connect with nature's rhythm in its purest form. The Masurian landscape is a wonder to behold, with its intricate network of lakes and waterways. It beckons travellers to embark on a voyage of discovery and exploration, offering solace in simplicity. The echoes of history whisper through the rustling leaves while ancient castles stand as silent sentinels of bygone eras. Every breath of crisp, clean air attunes one to the harmony of the land, where every sunrise paints a new masterpiece across the canvas of the sky. Time stands still in Masuria, offering a sanctuary for the weary soul and a haven for the wanderer in search of serenity. Experience the captivating beauty of Masuria, a realm of lakes and legends that will transport you to a world of tranquillity, history, and beauty. Masuria is a region that offers an abundance of lakes and forests for outdoor activities and boasts of cultural heritage. Similarly, Shropshire has many historical sites and varied landscapes to explore.

Masuria's economy is based on tourism and agriculture, while Shropshire thrives on a combination of agriculture, manufacturing, and tourism. Both regions are known for their natural beauty and historical charm, making them admirable tourist destinations. The similarities between Masuria in Poland and Shropshire are obvious. Both regions share a common essence despite their geographical separation. Masuria is renowned for its beautiful lakes and forests, while Shropshire is blessed with rolling hills and winding rivers. The landscapes of both regions speak to the timeless allure of nature's embrace. In Masuria, history whispers through ancient ruins, while Shropshire echoes with the footsteps of centuries past. Its storied castles and quaint villages serve as testaments to a bygone era. However, beyond the surface, it is the intangible essence of both regions that truly brings them together. They share a sense of tranquillity, reverence for tradition, and an unwavering spirit of community, inviting you to become a part of their story. In Masuria and Shropshire, one can find not just picturesque landscapes but also a sanctuary for the soul. It's a place where time stands still, and the heart finds peace in the genuine beauty of the world.

The Polish community in Shropshire has a rich history that dates back to World War II. After the war, numerous Polish refugees and their families settled in the Shropshire region of England, and one significant event was the establishment of the Tilstock Camp, also known as Higher Heath. Initially, this camp was used as an internment camp for Austrian and German refugees during World War II, but it was later converted into an RAF airfield in 1942. After the war, it provided temporary accommodation to Polish refugees and their families as they rebuilt their lives. There were other camps in Cannock, Staffordshire that also assisted survivors who had lost everything due to the impact of Stalinism and Nazism. Publications such as "A Concise History of Poland" by Jerzy Lukowski provide an overview of Polish history, including the experiences of Polish people in the UK after World War II. Following Victory in Europe Day, many Polish families who had been held captive in Siberian or German work camps were released. With no homes to return to due to the fact that their land had now been absorbed into Russia, they were transported across Persia to Africa, where they resided for several years before landing in England.

Polish families integrated into British society in market towns such as Wellington by preserving their own culture while respecting the host country's culture and laws. When this was achieved, it produced a strong sense of cohesion that benefited all those concerned. The first wave of Polish immigrants after WW2 had managed to survive the Molotov-Ribbentrop Pact, Monte Cassino, and Communist rule, to name but a few. In Wellington, the first generation worked at places such as Sankey's and continued to be inspired by the Polish Catholic work ethic. Polish traditions represent a vibrant tapestry woven from centuries of antiquity, rich cultural heritage, and a zest for life that is evident in every celebration. These traditions reflect the resilience and spirit of the Polish people and include both solemn religious rituals and lively festivals. At the core of Polish tradition lies the importance of family, with gatherings often focused on rustic meals featuring dishes like *pierogi* (dumplings), *bigos* (hunter's stew), and *paczki* (filled doughnuts). These culinary delights aren't just food but also a symbol of Polish hospitality and the warmth of shared moments.

Religious customs remain significant in Polish life, with holidays such as Christmas and Easter celebrated with great enthusiasm. During Wigilia (Christmas Eve), families gather for a feast of twelve traditional dishes, each representing a different aspect of the holiday. In some cases, individuals will not begin eating until they see the first star in the sky! One of the quirkiest Polish traditions is the annual *Śledzik*, or "Herring Night," where friends and family come together to feast on an abundance of pickled herring, vodka, and lively conversation. This tradition may seem unusual to outsiders, but it embodies the Polish love for socialising, good food, and embracing life's simple pleasures. In Poland, tradition is not just about preserving the past but also about embracing, enriching, and passing it on to future generations. It's a celebration of identity, a source of pride, and a reminder that amidst the fast pace of modern life, there's always time to pause, reflect, and honour the customs that connect our roots. Polish children growing up in Britain often find themselves living with one foot in Polish culture and the other in British culture. This gives them a fascinating blend of traditions, languages, and experiences. From a young age, they learn to navigate these two worlds, seamlessly weaving together the customs and values of their Polish heritage and British surroundings.

At home, Polish children immerse themselves in their traditions, language, and cuisine. Polish is spoken at the dinner table, and trips to Poland to visit relatives are cherished opportunities to connect with different parts of the family. However, outside the home, these children are part of British society. They attend school, make friends, and engage with the local community. They navigate the complexities of language and culture, learning to adapt and find common ground while embracing their differences. Growing up with dual cultural identities can be enriching and inspiring, offering these children a broader perspective on the world and many useful insights. But there can also be challenges, and navigating the expectations and norms of both cultures can be daunting, requiring these children to forge their path and define their sense of self.

In 2004, Poland joined the European Union, leading to a second wave of Polish families moving to this country in search of a better life. The Polish community in Wellington, Shropshire, has become integral to the town's cultural and social fabric, thriving through its second and third generations. At the top of the town, a Polish bakery and supermarket warmly welcome visitors, offering authentic cuisine that has won Wellington's residents' hearts and taste buds, creating a shared culinary heritage that bridges cultures. In fact, the excellent *Masovia Craft Bakery* at the top of New Street is a great place to discover the delights of freshly baked treats, bread, pastries and amazing cakes. The community's dedication to education and entrepreneurship has also significantly impacted the town's development, with Polish-led initiatives contributing to local schools and businesses. Polish language classes and cultural workshops ensure that younger generations remain connected to their roots while embracing their British identities. As Wellington looks ahead, the enduring spirit and contributions of the Polish community continue to inspire and uplift, promising a future where every cultural thread is woven into a shared, vibrant narrative. Meanwhile, 1219 miles away, Masuria shares its natural beauty, cultural heritage, and welcoming atmosphere, making it an attractive destination for travellers seeking an escape to a version of Shropshire's beautiful countryside.

Get ready to tantalize your taste buds with the irresistible delights of Polish cuisine! From the mouthwatering pierogi, filled with delectable ingredients like potatoes, cheese, and fruit, to the indulgent pączki doughnuts that are a must-have on *Fat Thursday*, Polish culinary traditions are a thrill for your palate. Savour the velvety Sernik cheesecake and the heavenly makowiec poppy seed roll, and dive into the rich and savoury kielbasa sausages and the comforting gołąbki cabbage rolls. But that's not all - don't miss out on the zesty zapiekanka street food and the unique oscypek smoked sheep cheese. And for the perfect finale, treat yourself to the crispy chruściki pastries and the luscious kremówka cream cake. Get ready for a culinary adventure and to experience some Polish hospitality.

Throughout its storied history, Wellington has also welcomed people from many different cultures, with each contributing their unique culinary flavours to the town. The collective influence has bestowed an irresistible charm on this area, and the food court's popularity in the old market is evidence of this. However, in this chapter, I have chosen to explore the cultural influence that has left an indelible mark on my soul - the vibrant and hospitable Polish community. Growing up amidst their warmth and traditions has profoundly shaped my worldview and made it an honour to pay homage to their enduring legacy within these pages. Through their resilience, generosity, and unwavering spirit, the Polish community has enriched Wellington and contributed towards its revival. Dziękuję za wszystko

Chapter Eight
Saturday Morning Rituals

Saturday shopping is more than just a practical task - it's a ritual that involves relaxation, rejuvenation, and connection with the world outside our daily routines. As Saturday rolls around, you have the opportunity to indulge in the timeless tradition of shopping and allow it to brighten your weekend by visiting a market town. Saturday shopping holds a special place in the hearts of many people. It's a time when the hustle and bustle of the workweek fade away, and the promise of leisure and exploration beckons. For some, Saturday shopping is a cherished tradition, a weekly ritual that brings joy and excitement. Whether it's strolling through a market, hunting for bargains, or browsing in a record store, Saturdays are reserved for indulging in multiple pleasures. During my childhood, Saturdays were devoted to visiting Wellington and partaking in a weekly tradition. These seemingly ordinary activities held profound significance, serving as valuable life lessons. They taught me to appreciate the importance of small things and how they can rival the significance of grand events. As I reflected upon these aspects, I came to understand the interconnectedness of life and its unique rhythm. Saturday traditions served as more than just routines; they were moments that I still cherish.

Saturday Morning Ritual One: Wellington, here we come!

On Saturday mornings, my father and I used to drive to Wellington in our family car, a *Standard Vanguard*. These journeys were special and enabled me to have conversations with my father about his family's history. He was a hard-working man with an inventor's mind who was always making things. We always parked opposite the *Chad Valley* Factory and would walk into Wellington together, enjoying the sights and sounds of a busy town. Our Saturday morning routine always began at the top of New Street. The first stop was always the butcher's shop, where there were always humorous conversations. Across the street, there was a boutique adorned with a poster of a bullfighter, evoking vivid images of the Spanish countryside in my mind. At the end of New Street, there was a shop filled with an array of household goods belonging to my father's friend, Gino. Further down the street, *Woolworths* dominated the scene. It was a bustling emporium where my parents indulged my passion for music by purchasing my first amplifier. Wellington was extremely busy on Saturday mornings in those days, and traffic flowed through the town. People conversed in groups, and some would attend a football match at the *Bucks Head* to watch Telford United. There is a strong football tradition in the area, as the winning England World Cup team of 1966 trained at Lilleshall before their historic victory. Several years later, their famous goalkeeper Gordon Banks assumed the role of manager at Telford United, but his tenure was not successful, and I remember seeing him leaving the ground in his car one day with a worried look on his face. It's funny the things you remember.

At this point in our Saturday morning ritual, my father and I would separate to complete our various duties. There was always someone from the Polish community who would stop my father for a chat. Wellington was the main town in the area, so the market was always crowded on Saturday mornings. It was the same for all the market towns in Shropshire, such as Shrewsbury, Market Drayton, Ludlow, Much Wenlock, and Church Stretton. In the outside area of the market, there was a large stall selling plates with ornate designs, and the trader was a memorable raconteur. He would engage the public using emotive language before encouraging them to purchase his items. I can still hear him now whenever I am in that corner of the market.

"Not one...not two...but three for the price of one!"

In another corner of the outdoor market, there was a covered second-hand bookstall filled with used books on a variety of topics, including history, astronomy, philosophy, and psychology. The covers of the science fiction paperbacks transported readers to other worlds and introduced abstract ideas on other planets. I always wanted one of my books to grace those shelves one day, but the stall is gone, and I'm on Amazon now!

Saturday Morning Ritual Two: Walton's Music Shop

Another Saturday morning ritual involved music lessons at *Walton's Music Shop* on Tan Bank in Wellington. My accordion lessons with the talented Anita Barber were always a highlight. Anita's teaching style was unique, combining traditional accordion music with modern song transcriptions. Her passion for music was contagious, and she had a way of making even the most challenging parts of the music seem achievable. The music shop itself was a treasure trove of vintage guitars and amplifiers, including rare pieces like the *Hagstrom Sparkle*, a stunning space-age guitar that still captivates me to this day. The shop was owned by Edith Walton and managed by her son, Brian, a gifted musician with his own band called *The Earls*. I remember the excitement of performing annually at *Oakengates Town Hall* as part of the *Edith Walton Accordion Show Band*. It was there that I had my first taste of playing in a full theatre, and it was an unforgettable experience. The concert was also a special occasion because my favourite primary school teacher, William Marston, was in the audience. After the performance, he surprised me with a soft drink, even though I asked him for a whisky! Those were truly magical days filled with music, learning, and notable experiences.

Saturday Morning Ritual Three: The Clifton Cinema

I vividly remember the electrifying Saturday morning ritual of visiting the *Clifton cinema* in Wellington. The atmosphere was always charged with anticipation and nostalgia as we made our way through familiar landmarks and bustling shops towards the cinema. The sight of vintage movie posters in the foyer added to the thrill of the cinematic experience, and the usherettes, with their discreet torches, guided us to our seats, exuding an air of glamour and excitement. I can still recall the palpable sense of community and familiarity as we settled in for a cinematic adventure. As the lights dimmed and the curtains parted, the collective silence in the auditorium was almost tangible. It was here that I first experienced the magic of the big screen, with breathtaking aerial shots sweeping over the hills of Switzerland, introducing the voice of Julie Andrews. I was also captivated by the depth of tone created by multiple double basses in John

Barry's music and witnessed Goldfinger's dastardly attempts to outsmart James Bond. As a teenager, I enjoyed going to the movies in the evening with my friend, where we were transported to worlds of adventure, beauty, and even horror. Those were the days of excitement, discovery, and missed opportunities such as the time my friend and I stood next to two attractive girls in the queue at another cinema in the town called *The Grand* but were too shy to start a conversation. I often wonder where they are now. The memories of those enchanting cinema experiences will always hold a special place in my heart.

Saturday rituals in Wellington were always great fun! Planning out the day felt like embarking on an exciting adventure. Even though Wellington has changed over time, there are still new places waiting to be discovered. The best part is that you can create your own Saturday morning traditions, contribute to the revival of a market town, and connect with some fascinating business owners. By blending shopping with meaningful conversations and making connections with local entrepreneurs, this ritual not only boosts the local economy but also nurtures a strong sense of community and gratitude for the people behind the products. It turns shopping into a rewarding and unforgettable experience for everyone involved. Here are some rituals that you might want to experience for yourself:

Farmers' Market Feast: Start your Saturday with an extraordinary shopping adventure - dive into the lively ambience of *Wellington Market*! Explore stalls brimming with fresh farm produce, artisanal cheeses, and homemade preserves. Connect with local entrepreneurs and producers, savouring their creations and uncovering the stories behind their goods. Finish off your adventure by selecting top-quality ingredients for a farm-to-table feast, ensuring an unmatched and genuine culinary journey!

Café Crawl Delight: Embark on an exhilarating café adventure through Wellington's historic streets, immersing yourself in the town's rich coffee culture and savouring delectable delights. Kick off your journey with a luxurious cappuccino as you and your loved ones enjoy laughter and games at *The Gaming Cafe*, surrounded by the enticing aroma of freshly ground beans. Then, tantalize your taste buds with exquisite pastries, cakes, a custom-made sandwich, and a cup of herbal tea. Finally, conclude your café crawl by unwinding at another coffee shop, ordering a Cappuccino and a tasty brunch while soaking in the lively ambience and engaging conversation at the *Gratitude Café*.

Harmony of Strings: Immerse yourself in a musical wonderland with a special ritual dedicated to finding the perfect musical instrument in Wellington! Explore the town's one-of-a-kind music store, *The Guitar Vault*, which houses an extraordinary collection of guitars, amps and pedals. Take your time to test out different models and experience the resonance of each note as you pluck the strings. Engage with friendly staff who can offer expert guidance and tailored recommendations to match your musical style and expertise. Conclude your ritual by choosing the instrument that will ignite your musical journey!

Tapas Trail Adventure: Embark on an epic culinary adventure through the vibrant streets of Wellington and immerse yourself in the rich flavours of Spain with a thrilling tapas trail experience! Prepare to tantalize your taste buds at *The Orange House*, where you'll savour an array of mouthwatering traditional tapas dishes bursting with authenticity and flavour. From the classic favourites like patatas bravas, and chorizo al vino to the tantalizing gambas al ajillo, all paired with a glass of refreshing sangria or crisp Spanish wine. Get ready to savour each delectable bite and revel in the shared experience of communal dining. Get set for an unforgettable journey of culinary delights!

Rituals play a crucial role in society by fostering a sense of continuity and structure, which are essential for maintaining social cohesion and cultural identity. Through rituals, communities can celebrate their shared history, values, and traditions, thereby reinforcing a collective memory that spans generations. These practices, whether religious, cultural, or social, provide a predictable framework within which individuals can find stability and meaning amidst the flux of everyday life. By marking significant life events, seasonal changes, and communal milestones, rituals help individuals navigate transitions and maintain a sense of order and purpose. In essence, rituals act as anchors, grounding people in their heritage while guiding them through the present and into the future, thereby ensuring the persistence and resilience of societal norms and connections.

Totnes in Devon, England, comes alive every Saturday morning with a dynamic fusion of historical traditions and modern community activities. Imagine a vibrant market brimming with local produce, handmade crafts, antiques, and mouth-watering street food, drawing both locals and visitors. This centuries-old tradition not only supports local businesses but also fosters a strong sense of community and continuity as residents and visitors gather to engage in commerce, socialize, and uphold a tradition that links the present to the past. But that's not all! Totnes also embraces modern Saturday morning rituals, becoming a hub for sustainability and alternative living. Yoga classes, community workshops, and eco-friendly initiatives often attract a diverse group of participants and promote a lifestyle focused on health, well-being, and environmental consciousness. These activities complement the traditional market, offering a holistic approach to community life that honours the past while embracing the future. And the impact? These Saturday morning rituals significantly boost the local economy by generating substantial footfall and creating a thriving environment for local businesses. The consistent flow of people not only sustains existing enterprises but also encourages new ventures, fostering economic growth and innovation. It's a win-win for everyone involved! In the aftermath of the COVID-19 pandemic, new Saturday morning traditions have emerged, such as outdoor fitness classes and farmers' markets with enhanced safety measures. These new rituals help rebuild community connections and stimulate the local economy, providing a sense of normalcy and recovery and helping towns like Totnes adapt and thrive in a post-pandemic world. Totnes is a shining example of how blending tradition and modernity can not only preserve the cultural fabric of a town but also drive its economic prosperity. It's a celebration of community spirit, innovation, and resilience, showcasing the multifaceted benefits of maintaining and evolving community rituals. A Community spirit that continues to make itself known in Wellington, Shropshire.

In market towns like Wellington, rituals are woven into the very fabric of life, playing a central and essential role. These rituals passed down through generations, serve as anchors in times of uncertainty, providing a sense of continuity and community. For example, the weekly market is more than just a place to buy and sell goods; it's a cherished tradition that brings people together, fostering connections and camaraderie. The familiar rhythm of market day, with its bustling stalls and lively atmosphere, offers a reassuring sense In an ever-changing world, rituals provide a sense of normalcy. During times of crisis, these rituals become even more important, serving as symbols of resilience and solidarity. The market becomes a beacon of hope where neighbours can come together to support one another and reaffirm their shared values. Whether it's the annual harvest festival or the festive Christmas market, these events remind us of the strength of community bonds and the power of collective action. In Shropshire, rituals in market towns are crucial, weaving the fabric of community life, binding people together, and providing a sense of belonging. As the region continues to navigate the challenges of the post-pandemic era, these rituals will play a crucial role in building resilience, developing a sense of purpose, and ensuring that places like Wellington remain a place of warmth, welcome, and enduring tradition.

Chapter Nine

The Doughnut Effect

A business theory known as *The Doughnut Effect*, first developed in America, explains how the development of out-of-town businesses causes the centre of a town to become empty, creating a doughnut-like effect. This theory gained popularity as the impact of such businesses began to have a negative impact on small towns. Executives from around the world began to follow this approach because of its potential to generate profits. In the 1970s and 80s, this kind of business model began to significantly impact Wellington as the outskirts of the town began to be developed, causing its once-vibrant centre to feel the full force of the 'Doughnut Effect '. This resulted in a significant reduction in footfall and a general sense of emptiness at the heart of the community. However, from the beginning, there was a determined effort to defend Wellington and reduce any unnecessary closures. The beginnings of this situation can be traced back to a specific event that can be summed up in one word:

Carrefour!

At that time, a new shopping experience named *Carrefour* arrived like a spaceship from France. Its introduction of the hypermarket concept to the region was a game-changer, marking a significant event in the town's history. People flocked to this exciting shopping experience, which also offered free parking. Carrefour, a modern hypermarket, quickly became a popular destination for locals. It was built in Telford New Town and opened in October 1973 as part of phase one of a larger development. *Queen Elizabeth II* inaugurated phase two in 1981. My parents were present at that time and saw the Queen in her beautiful green outfit. Her Majesty was once asked what it was like to be royal and apparently replied, "Everywhere you go, it smells of fresh paint!" I'm sure that there was a whiff of Dulux in the air on that particular occasion and that everything was *de rigueur*, as the French like to say. The arrival of *Carrefour* at *Telford Shopping Centre*, as it was called then, heralded a new era for small market towns such as Wellington. Over the next few years, footfall in the town began to noticeably reduce in numbers as the novelty and convenience of shopping at the new Hypermarket began to supersede market town activities. The once-vibrant centre of Wellington now felt the full force of the 'Doughnut Effect ', with a significant reduction in footfall and a general sense of emptiness at the heart of the community. From a French perspective, the idea of opening *Carrefour* outlets on British soil was a bold move and part of an ambitious strategy that included other locations in the South of England and Wales.

Carrefour is a French word meaning "Crossroads", which is where the business first operated in 1960, within the suburb of Annecy. It then developed from a shop into a hypermarket and quickly became a pioneer in the retail industry, known for its vast selection of goods, competitive prices, and innovative shopping experience. As it expanded beyond French borders, Telford became one of the early destinations for *Carrefour*'s international ventures. The arrival of *Carrefour* in Telford brought a wave of excitement, offering locals access to a diverse range of products and a taste of continental shopping culture. With its modern facilities and customer-centric approach,

Carrefour soon became a popular fixture in the community, shaping the retail landscape of Telford for decades to come.

As other businesses opened branches at the shopping centre, the centre of Wellington began to suffer the effects of this change. At that time, *Carrefour* represented the *zeitgeist*, the spirit of the age, and an early example of successful out-of-town shopping. One important factor of *Carrefour*'s success was the free parking it offered, which was later replaced by a payment method that remains unpopular to this day. Entering *Carrefour* was akin to stepping into a treasure trove of gastronomic delights. The air was filled with the scent of freshly baked Tiger bread, mingling with ripe fruits and exotic spices. The shelves were adorned with an array of goods, each one promising a taste of something new and exciting. Among the myriad of items lining the aisles, one could find packets of *Gypsy Cream* biscuits and *Old Jamaica* chocolate bars. *Carrefour*'s delights extended far beyond its biscuits and chocolate bars with an assortment of goods, from pantry staples like tins of beans and packets of pasta to exotic delicacies sourced from far-flung corners of the globe. There was once a small shark for sale on the fish counter, which was an interesting way to attract customers. This illustrates how *Carrefour* always had something going on and how it managed to sustain the interest of customers.

All these elements combined to produce a veritable feast for the senses, with each product offering a tantalising promise of flavour and satisfaction. As shoppers navigated the aisles of *Carrefour*, their family sized trolleys filled with an assortment of goods, they were greeted by friendly and helpful staff, ready to assist with any inquiries or recommendations. This fascinating story takes us back to 1937 when an American entrepreneur named Sylvan Goldman revolutionized the shopping experience forever. As the owner of the *Humpty Dumpty Supermarket* chain in Oklahoma, he introduced the concept of shopping trolleys with larger baskets and manoeuvrable wheels, transforming the industry forever. This innovation not only gave customers more control but also made using shopping trolleys fashionable. The glitz and glamour of the *Carrefour* shopping experience were further enhanced by regular appearances from soap stars of the day. However, despite its initial impact, the Hypermarket experience could not be sustained, leading to strategic shifts and the eventual departure of the French from the scene. C'était bien pendant que cela durait (it was good while it lasted).

Carrefour's departure from *Telford Shopping Centre* was a strategic decision amidst shifting market trends and increased competition. The company opted to invest in innovative concepts like *Carrefour Planet* in Western Europe, reflecting its commitment to staying ahead in the retail game. This decision marked a broader shift in the company's strategy to drive growth and maintain relevance in an ever-changing retail landscape. I once visited a *Carrefour* on the outskirts of Paris, and it was similar to any other midrange supermarket...but back then, it was the future, and many customers loved it. However, you can get sick of doughnuts! By that time, of course, many businesses had been attracted to the Telford shopping centre, and the impact of the doughnut effect was being felt by Wellington and many other market towns in Shropshire. In recent times, the doughnut effect has been tackled due to the support of *The Council*, *Love Wellington*, and a group of determined business owners. Interestingly, the pandemic has also increased footfall in Wellington by encouraging customers to discover a range of established and innovative new niche businesses. Ironically, the rise of online shopping during the pandemic has led to a reduction in foot traffic in developments outside market towns, while the opposite has occurred in the centre of the towns. We may be witnessing the emergence of a *reverse* doughnut effect from a historical perspective. Remember where you heard it first!

In the 1970s, there was widespread excitement about the future, as it promised a technological revolution. Society stood on the brink of unprecedented change, embracing the dawn of a new era where innovation and progress intertwined. From the advent of personal computing to the birth of the internet, the future seemed full of possibilities, beckoning all to embark on a journey of transformation together. Amidst cultural shifts and political upheavals, there was a unifying sense of anticipation as individuals from all walks of life eagerly awaited the unfolding of a shared destiny shaped by the accelerating march of technology. However, in England, the dream of the 1970s began to fade due to a confluence of economic, social, and political challenges. In the early part of the decade, the nation had a lot of optimism. This changed as the country faced economic instability. The oil crisis of 1973 caused energy prices to rise, leading to inflation and putting pressure on households and businesses. There was also a lot of industrial unrest, with strikes and labour disputes that disrupted society and eroded confidence in the government's ability to manage the economy. Social tensions were also on the rise due to increasing unemployment and a widening gap between the rich and poor.

The decline of traditional industries, such as manufacturing and mining, left many communities struggling with unemployment and poverty, which made a lot of people feel alienated and disappointed with the government. Politically, the 1970's were marked by a series of crises and scandals that eroded public trust in the establishment. The Conservative government of Edward During the 1970s, England experienced significant challenges that culminated in *The Winter of Discontent* 1978-1979. This period was characterized by widespread strikes and social unrest. The resulting upheaval paved the way for the election of Margaret Thatcher and the rise of neoliberal policies in the 1980s, marking a significant departure from the social and economic ethos of the previous decade. The fading of the 1970s dream in England can be attributed to a combination of economic instability, social tensions, and political upheaval, which collectively undermined the optimism and sense of possibility that had characterized the early part of the decade. During this time, *Carrefour* made its appearance in the town centre, and more and more out-of-town developments emerged. At the same time, numerous businesses in Wellington demonstrated resilience in overcoming the challenges posed by that situation, with some successfully enduring to the present day. The level of investment and expansion beyond Wellington during that era was remarkable, signifying a new chapter in retail shopping. However, that trend gradually shifted with the advent of the internet, as people changed their shopping habits once again.

Amidst the resurgence of local markets and community gatherings, supermarkets and hypermarkets now face unprecedented challenges. The shift in consumer behaviour brought about by the pandemic, including increased reliance on online shopping and concerns about overcrowded indoor spaces, has led to declining footfall in these retail giants. Furthermore, supply chain disruptions and rising operational costs have strained their ability to meet changing demands and maintain competitive pricing. The opening of *Carrefour* on the outskirts of Wellington demonstrated the natural shifts that take place in a competitive market. Initially, the new retail giant drew shoppers away from the town centre, affecting local foot traffic and economic activity. However, over time, a balance has emerged, allowing customers to benefit from both large supermarkets and local shops. Embracing both options allows people to enjoy the convenience and variety offered by supermarkets while also investing in the prosperity and resilience of their local area. Nonetheless, there are those who believe that supporting local businesses is now more important than ever, as it helps sustain local economies and build community spirit. Additionally, local businesses often offer personalized services and unique products that large chains cannot match, enriching the overall shopping experience. Shopping locally contributes to the vitality and uniqueness of market towns, and the more we visit them, the better they become!

Chapter Ten

The Edge of Chaos

"The Edge of Chaos" is not just a theory but a practical tool for managing complex situations. It suggests that the best way to navigate such a situation is to be as creative and adaptable as possible. This theory, like tending a garden that is not too controlled or not too chaotic, offers the opportunity to create something special. It's a call to action, a reminder that there is always room for creativity and innovation, even in the most challenging situations. This theory can be used to manage a wide variety of things, including the way in which a market town can survive. A useful way to illustrate this is by looking at the way in which a group of individuals, local councillors and the government successfully revived Wellington, demonstrating the power of creativity and adaptability in managing complex situations.

The 'Edge of Chaos' is a term that has been used in academia for several years. It describes a situation where things are almost lost…but not quite. It suggests that the 'edge of chaos' is a space in which we can use creativity to find a solution to a problem, inspiring hope and potential. This concept, which emerged in the late 20th century, particularly in the field of theoretical physics and complexity science, is not just a theoretical construct but a practical tool for managing complex situations. It gained prominence in the 1980s and 1990s through the groundbreaking work of scientists such as Stuart Kauffman, Brian Arthur, and John B Holland. These researchers explored the dynamics of complex systems and the behaviour of nonlinear systems, highlighting the transition states where systems exhibit both *order* and *chaos*. This marked a shift in understanding in relation to complex systems, sparking a surge of interest in complexity theory across various disciplines, including biology, economics, and social sciences, as scholars sought to understand the underlying principles governing complex phenomena. The notion of the 'edge of chaos' became a central concept in complexity theory, illustrating the critical balance between stability and adaptability within complex systems. We can use this to understand many things, including how a market town works.

The challenges faced during Wellington's revival were significant. By the 1990s, the impact of out-of-town shopping developments had taken its toll on what had previously been a busy market town. The town had seen a decrease in foot traffic and the closure of numerous well-established businesses. The town now featured multiple charity shops, creating a general impression of a decline in its former status. One of the ideas being discussed at that time was the possibility that some towns might disappear altogether and have their buildings converted into housing. It was difficult to recognize Wellington as it had been in the 1960s during its heyday, when people dressed up to visit, reflecting an important aspect of Shropshire life. It would be fair to say that during this time, Wellington was taken to the "edge of chaos". However, the town had strong roots that date back over a thousand years and several groups and forward-thinking individuals who decided to challenge this decline. The changes that took place in Wellington at that time were influenced by the relocation of a major shopping centre three miles away. This trend was multiplied many times across the country, and in each case, there was an opportunity to use creativity to face the challenges that this new situation presented. However, no one said it was going to be easy or that it could be accomplished overnight! Now let's have a look at someone whose life work involved putting this theory into action and how she made it happen.

Professor Brenda Zimmerman was a prominent scholar in organisational studies from New York who was renowned for her contributions to complexity theory and leadership. Her work is based on reducing complexity within organisations, focusing on navigating *uncertainty* and promoting *resilience*. This is evident in the co-development of the *Cynefin framework*, which categorised problems into *simple, complicated, complex,* and *chaotic* domains, guiding decision-making based on their complexity. In the context of organisational leadership, Brenda Zimmerman advocated adaptive approaches that embraced uncertainty and enabled organisations to thrive in dynamic environments. Applying these theories to a market town such as Wellington illustrates the way in which it survived commercial annihilation through a similar approach. As the town began to respond to the allure of out-of-town developments drawing commerce away from its traditional business model, it found itself on the edge of chaos. However, as I have explained, a collective spirit and creative thinking led to the emergence of several opportunities for an adaptive response. Inspired by similar ideas, community leaders and stakeholders rallied to embrace the seriousness of the situation and found innovative solutions to revive the town and preserve its identity. The town successfully addressed its issues through the collaborative efforts of individuals and authorities, utilizing creative thinking to find solutions. This approach proved effective, allowing Wellington to showcase the pivotal role of creativity in managing chaos and ultimately transforming the town into an attractive destination for shopping once more.

As Wellington navigated this boundary, it found itself on the brink of profound change, poised to embrace chaos as a catalyst for its revival. With the sudden arrival of the COVID-19 pandemic, a tidal wave of uncertainty swept across the globe, bringing with it an unprecedented era of disruption and upheaval. As countries grappled with the rapidly escalating crisis, stringent lockdown measures were swiftly implemented, bringing daily life to a grinding halt. The once-bustling streets of towns and cities fell silent, businesses closed their doors, and social interactions abruptly stopped. In this new reality, people found themselves isolated, grappling with an overwhelming sense of fear and apprehension for the future. The spectre of the virus loomed large, casting a shadow of uncertainty over every aspect of daily existence. For many, the pandemic evoked echoes of the collective trauma experienced during the Second World War, as a pervasive sense of vulnerability and mortality pervaded society. In this unprecedented moment, the world was united in a shared experience of fear and uncertainty as individuals grappled with the profound implications of a global crisis unlike any other.

Throughout the pandemic, the businesses in Wellington showed incredible initiative, finding ways to operate and deliver services within imposed parameters. This response highlighted the strength of local connections and the power of collective action. Systems within systems. Despite the challenges, Wellington proved remarkably resilient, with its historic Market becoming an important point of contact and Anthony's of Wellington Farm Shop & Coffee providing multiple services. The robustness of Wellington during the pandemic was severely tested, as it was in all of the market towns in Shropshire and beyond. During this time, Wellington was again taken to the "edge of chaos" as the world plunged into enforced hibernation and collective deep thinking. Wellington successfully navigated the edge of chaos twice and addressed its challenges effectively.

It is interesting to note that Brenda Zimmerman was particularly interested in ways to reduce complexity within healthcare systems. *The Princess Royal Hospital* near Wellington was also driven to the "edge of chaos" during the pandemic and faced an overwhelming demand on its resources. However, there was an effective use of creative thinking to reduce the damage that such a situation could cause. This was evident in the management of beds and the dedication of the healthcare professionals who worked so hard and continue to do so. In the intricate workings of complex systems – from Hospitals and bustling cities to historic market towns, there is a sweet spot where structure meets flexibility. Here, rules are not rigid shackles but rather gentle guidelines, offering just enough stability to encourage innovation while allowing room for spontaneity. But what makes this zone so special? It's all about finding the perfect harmony. Too much order stifles creativity, locking people into old routines and stifling new ideas. On the other hand, too much chaos leads to confusion and disarray, making progress nearly impossible. At the Edge of Chaos, however, lies a playground of possibility. It's a place where diverse perspectives collide, failure is seen as a stepping stone rather than a stumbling block, and innovation thrives in the face of uncertainty - where creativity reigns supreme!

In the future, Wellington can encourage and support local initiatives and community-driven solutions to promote self-organization. This approach empowers residents, businesses, and civic organizations to adapt and innovate in response to changing needs and circumstances. Initiatives such as community gardens, local entrepreneurship programs, and neighbourhood revitalization projects can thrive under such conditions, contributing to the overall vitality of the town. Additionally, Wellington can enhance its resilience by diversifying its economic base, strengthening social networks, and investing in infrastructure that improves connectivity. A diverse economy reduces risks associated with dependence on single industries and encourages innovation and adaptability. Strengthening social networks through initiatives like community events, neighbourhood associations, and collaborative projects builds trust and social capital, enabling residents to support each other during times of need. In the field of business, chaos theory also represents a delicate equilibrium between order and disorder. It suggests that systems operating at this boundary can achieve success by allowing for *adaptability* and *innovation* while maintaining a level of stability. Imagine a business environment where things are neither too rigid nor too chaotic. Instead, they exist in a state of controlled turbulence, where creativity flourishes and new ideas can emerge. This balance encourages resilience, enabling enterprises to respond effectively to unforeseen challenges and opportunities.

At the edge of chaos, businesses embrace change as a constant, recognising that static structures can hinder growth while excessive disorder leads to instability. By operating within this dynamic zone, organisations can navigate uncertainties with agility, seizing opportunities for growth and evolution. In essence, the edge of chaos theory offers a framework for businesses to thrive in an ever-evolving landscape where the only constant is change. It encourages companies to embrace complexity, adaptability, and innovation as essential for success in today's competitive environment. This theory is exemplified in the story of Wellington's revival, a town that faced economic decline but managed to reinvent itself by embracing change and innovation. Amidst this idyllic scene lies a dramatic twist - a revelation that the edge of chaos, far from being a place of uncertainty, is where true revival occurs. Wellington found its strength, courage, and hope in the face of adversity. On the edge of chaos, the true spirit of the community was revealed, and leaders came forward. And so, as the sun sets on the Wrekin, casting its golden glow upon the landscape, a new chapter begins - a chapter of revival, transformation, and triumph in the face of adversity.

Chapter Eleven

The Revival Begins

Love Wellington is an initiative supported by Telford & Wrekin Council and Wellington Council. Its aim is to attract visitors and businesses to the town. During my research for this book, Sally Themans from *Love Wellington* kindly sent me copies of *This is Our Wellington* magazine, which showcases the town's revitalization journey. The articles and pictures vividly portray how various individuals, business owners, the council, and government funding have collaborated to achieve this. The council's purchase of the market is an important milestone in the town's progress. The revitalization of market towns is a promising sign amidst the challenges of out-of-town development and the pandemic's impact. As the situation improves and we move into the endemic phase, people are eager to socialize outdoors again, and this hasn't changed. It's now up to the towns to organize events that will attract both tourists and locals.

The state of revival is characterized by a profound sense of renewal and rejuvenation, often following a period of stagnation or decline. It involves a surge of positive emotions, increased motivation, and a reinvigorated sense of purpose. People in this state typically feel a heightened sense of clarity and focus, enabling them to tackle life's challenges with renewed vigour. Revival can be triggered by various factors, such as personal achievements, new beginnings, or significant life changes, and it often leads to improved mental health and well-being. Ultimately, the state of revival fosters a resilient mindset, allowing individuals to embrace growth and transformation with optimism and enthusiasm. It's like a burst of energy and positivity after a period of feeling stuck or down. Revival can be sparked by achieving a personal goal, starting something new, or going through a big life change. It's like a mental and emotional reset button, and it can really improve overall well-being. When a community embraces revival, it's all about getting everyone involved and excited. This means supporting local projects, encouraging people to participate in community events, and ensuring everyone has access to essential services. Celebrating the community's unique culture, preserving the environment, and maintaining open communication between leaders and residents are essential for maintaining high levels of positive energy and community engagement. Sustaining a state of revival within a town involves fostering community engagement, supporting local projects, and promoting economic development. By encouraging active participation in local events and decision-making, the town can create a strong sense of belonging and investment in its future. Initiatives that address local needs, such as beautification efforts, cultural festivals, and sustainability projects, can boost communal pride and cooperation.

Access to quality education, healthcare, and recreational activities ensures residents' well-being and continuous growth. Celebrating local arts, culture, and heritage strengthens community identity, while environmental conservation enhances the town's aesthetics and sustainability. Transparent communication between officials and residents builds trust and encourages ongoing involvement, collectively contributing to the town's dynamic and positive atmosphere. Visitors, once attracted, often become loyal customers. Communities, with the active involvement of stakeholders, are realizing the inherent value of their town centres as places that foster a strong sense of identity and community. In response to sprawling developments, which can often dilute a town's unique character, local governments and residents are investing in revitalization efforts. These initiatives prioritize walkability, mixed-use zoning, and, importantly, the preservation of historic landmarks. The preservation of these landmarks serves as a testament to the town's rich history and a beacon of its resilience and adaptability. Towns are reclaiming their vitality by incentivizing businesses to establish themselves within town limits and creating vibrant public spaces. Such endeavours promote sustainable growth and cultivate a sense of pride and belonging among residents, fostering a renaissance that celebrates the rich tapestry of local culture and heritage. Importantly, these efforts also have a direct economic impact, as tourists who are attracted to the revitalized town become customers, contributing to the local economy.

Wellington's revitalization has genuinely rejuvenated the town, introducing an array of diverse businesses that add a unique flavour to its streets. As one enters from the top, the vibrant Polish businesses stand as a welcoming gateway, offering a tantalizing array of delights from their bakery and supermarket. Their presence not only adds a rich cultural dimension but also infuses the air with the aroma of freshly baked bread and the excitement of discovery. Beyond the Polish offerings, a mosaic of Eastern European businesses adds to the town's eclectic charm, each storefront telling a story of tradition and innovation. Walking down Main Street feels like stepping into a painting of optimism, where conversations intermingle with a gentle breeze carrying whispers of revitalization. It's a scene where locals and visitors alike can enjoy the simple joys of community, basking in the warmth of companionship amid the backdrop of Wellington's improved surroundings.

Wellington's revitalization is a physical transformation and a testament to its community's collective spirit and determination. As you stroll through the town from its free time-limited car parks, you're greeted not only by the promise of upcoming events but also by the palpable sense of pride and camaraderie among its residents. The Orbit Cinema, formerly a bank, is on the brink of a remarkable revival. With each passing day, it inches closer to its grand reopening, thanks to the tireless efforts of local volunteers and enthusiastic supporters. It has already proven to be a beacon of cultural enrichment, offering captivating films and a gathering place for cinephiles and numerous community groups. And let's not forget the tantalizing array of culinary delights awaiting patrons within the town. From sociable cafes to Mediterrancan cuisine, there is something to satisfy every palate, further enhancing the town's appeal as a destination for both locals and visitors. Meanwhile, the market scene in Wellington has undergone a significant transformation of its own. Once a traditional marketplace, it's now under the ownership and stewardship of the council, signalling a new era of community-driven initiatives and organic growth.

The addition of a lively food court has become a focal point for culinary adventures, showcasing the diverse flavours and cooking skills that define the region. As the sun sets, the market truly comes alive with the buzz of the night markets, where artisans, performers, and food vendors come together to create an unforgettable experience for all who wander through its bustling aisles. However, perhaps the most remarkable aspect of Wellington's resurgence lies in its physical amenities and the intangible sense of belonging that permeates every corner of the town. It's in the warm smiles exchanged between neighbours, the shared stories overheard at local cafes, and the collective sense of pride in how far the community has come. Indeed, the seeds of progress planted in the past few years are now bearing fruit, not just in the form of refurbished buildings and bustling markets, but in the renewed sense of hope and optimism that fills the air. As Wellington continues to evolve and thrive, its collective spirit will undoubtedly remain the driving force behind its ongoing success.

Let's not forget the potential for inspiring similar developments in other towns. Wellington, twinned with Châtenay-Malabry, both have unique histories that can serve as a catalyst for revivals. In recent years, Wellington has seen efforts towards regeneration, aiming to preserve its historical charm while adapting to modern needs. This revival often involves repurposing old industrial buildings into residential or commercial spaces, enhancing public areas, and promoting local businesses. The goal is typically to create a more vibrant town centre, attract tourists, and improve the quality of life for residents. Châtenay-Malabry, a suburb located just outside Paris, is known for its scientific institutions and research centres, including the École Polytechnique and the Institut Gustave Roussy. Recent developments in Châtenay-Malabry, influenced by its proximity to Paris and its role as a centre for education and research, have focused on improving transportation infrastructure, expanding educational facilities, and promoting innovation and collaboration within a scientific community.

Both towns, despite their geographic and cultural disparities, possess an astonishing ability to leverage their unique histories and cultural heritages to drive progress. Wellington exudes the charm of a market town with an industrial backdrop, while Chtenay-Malabry boasts scientific institutions and healthcare facilities. These communities exemplify how local identity and tradition can fuel improvement. Both places display a strong collective dedication to embracing change while preserving their distinctiveness. Rehabilitation entails not only reconstructing structures but also rejuvenating spirits and seizing potential. In France, the city of Saint-Étienne serves as a testament to the challenges involved in attempting a revival. Once a flourishing industrial centre, the city later confronted economic decline and urban decay. Despite efforts to invigorate the city, Saint-Étienne has faced numerous obstacles. One reason for these struggles is the absence of inclusive planning and community involvement. Revitalization efforts have faced criticism for prioritizing large-scale developments and corporate interests over the needs of local residents, raising concerns about gentrification and displacement. Without meaningful participation from all stakeholders, urban revivals risk alienating the very people they aim to benefit. The absence of comprehensive economic strategies has hindered Saint-Étienne's revival. Revitalization initiatives have primarily focused on attracting external investment and promoting tourism, neglecting the need to support local businesses and foster entrepreneurship. Furthermore, infrastructure deficiencies and environmental challenges have presented significant obstacles to Saint-Étienne's revival. The city's ageing infrastructure, transportation network, and public amenities require substantial investment and modernization. Environmental issues, such as air pollution and brownfield sites, further complicate efforts to attract investment and enhance the quality of life. Addressing infrastructure needs and environmental concerns is pivotal for Saint-Étienne's revival to thrive. Cities can teach towns valuable lessons, and this learning goes both ways. Cities can teach towns valuable lessons in terms of infrastructure development, economic strategies, and cultural diversity. The efficient public transportation systems, innovative business models, and vibrant arts scenes found in cities can serve as blueprints for towns looking to modernize and grow. Conversely, towns can offer cities insights into community cohesion, sustainable living, and preserving local traditions. This mutual exchange of knowledge and practices fosters a more balanced and enriching development for both urban and rural areas, highlighting the importance of interconnected growth and shared experiences.

Chapter Twelve

Electric Wellington

At 10:00 a.m. on a Thursday morning, the streets of Wellington hum with the gentle bustle of daily life. A man sporting a high-visibility jacket carefully parks a red electric delivery bicycle outside The Little Pantry, a popular refill shop in the town's heart. Inside, the shop's owner, Kelli King, springs into action as she prepares an order for one of her loyal customers. Meanwhile, another patron arrives, clutching a container eagerly awaiting to be filled with wholesome dry goods. However, The Little Pantry is more than just a shop; it's a beacon of a burgeoning movement towards sustainability and conscious living. It represents a social experiment aimed at reshaping consumer behaviour and promoting a sense of collective responsibility. With each refill and reuse; customers are not merely making purchases but a tangible contribution to a greener, more mindful way of life. As the electric delivery bicycle stands sentinel outside, it serves as a tangible reminder of the town's commitment to embracing change and charting a course towards a brighter, more sustainable future. With its innovative approach, The Little Pantry is not just a shop but a community-driven initiative that inspires us all to do our part and enjoy a new way to shop.

The atmosphere in the shop reminds me of "Original Unverpackt," a similar establishment in Berlin that I heard about a few years ago. It was established in 2014 by Milena Glimbovski and became the first store where customers could bring and refill their containers. The Little Pantry also reminds me of visits to The Centre For Alternative Technology in Machynlleth, Powys, in

Wales, during my youth. This was the first time I saw experiments in sustainable living in the days when there was more optimism attached to the idea and a celebration of what had been achieved already. Wellington is on the brink of a green future and is ready to embrace innovative solutions that reduce single-use plastic waste. This effort is complemented by a free delivery service provided by a team of volunteer cyclists, offering a friendly local service within a three-mile radius of the town. Wellington's council also acquired the aforementioned electric bicycle that symbolizes its commitment to green mobility solutions and encourages residents to reduce their carbon footprint by embracing alternative modes of transportation. In addition to conventional measures, Wellington is exploring creative eco-solutions and green spaces being utilised in several places, including the railway station. The town is establishing a path towards a sustainable and resilient future and a synthesis between environmental consciousness and traditional rural values. There are also other towns and cities that have successfully introduced such initiatives. Here are a few examples:

Freiburg is a charming city located in the southwestern region of Germany. It has earned the nickname of the "Green City" due to its unwavering commitment to promoting sustainable living. The city has taken several measures to achieve this goal, including the widespread use of solar panels on buildings, the creation of extensive bike lanes, and pedestrian-friendly zones. The Vauban neighbourhood is particularly noteworthy for its innovative car-free streets, energy-efficient buildings, and communal green spaces, all of which have helped to establish an eco-friendly and vibrant community. Copenhagen, the capital of Denmark, has emerged as a beacon of hope in the realm of sustainable urban development. The city has taken significant strides towards achieving carbon neutrality by 2025 with its Copenhagen Climate Plan. One of the key aspects of this plan is the promotion of cycling as the primary mode of transportation. The city boasts over two hundred miles of bike lanes and innovative infrastructure, such as a raised cycling bridge, which makes commuting easy. Furthermore, Copenhagen's commitment to renewable energy includes ambitious targets for wind power and district heating systems. Reykjavik, the capital of Iceland, is also renowned for its breathtaking natural beauty. Despite being a bustling capital city, it maintains a strong focus on sustainability and green living. Reykjavik's abundant geothermal resources provide the city with clean and renewable energy, which heats many homes and powers infrastructure. The city has ambitious goals for reducing carbon emissions and increasing green spaces. Its initiatives, such as urban farming and geothermal-heated outdoor swimming pools, contribute to its eco-friendly reputation and make it a truly unique place to live.

Japan is a country with a rich history of innovation, and it's no surprise that they've come up with some unique cycling delivery services that enliven everyday life. For example, in Tokyo, a Cat Café Bicycle Delivery service offers customers the opportunity to order drinks and snacks delivered by a staff member riding a bicycle decorated with adorable cat-themed designs. This is an excellent way to indulge in treats while also supporting a local business. In contrast, in Kyoto, Buddhist monks ride bicycles to deliver blessings to homes and businesses, adding a spiritual touch to the act of cycling and promoting harmony and well-being in the community. Other countries have also embraced the idea of cycling delivery services, each with its unique twist. In the Netherlands, florists offer bicycle delivery services, and skilled cyclists deliver fresh flower bouquets to customers' homes or workplaces, adding a touch of vibrancy to the transportation of their goods. Many companies are now exploring new ways to generate electricity by harnessing the kinetic energy produced by people as they move around a town or city. Cutting-edge technology is being developed to generate power when pedestrians walk past certain areas.

One such company is Pavegen, which specializes in kinetic energy harvesting technology. They have created innovative flooring systems that feature tiles equipped with electromagnetic generators. These tiles generate power as people walk across them, and the smart sensors and data analytics capabilities of Pavegen's product range provide sustainable energy solutions for various applications, from smart buildings to public spaces and transportation hubs. Energy-generating flooring tiles could be strategically installed in high-traffic areas, such as pedestrian walkways or public squares, to produce electricity that could power nearby streetlights and outdoor displays. Furthermore, Pavegen's smart sensor technology could be integrated into various infrastructure projects in Wellington. Public spaces could have sensors that collect data on foot traffic patterns, which could help city planners make informed decisions about urban design and resource allocation.

There is also a company called "SolePower", which specialises in energy harvesting and sustainability. They develop wearable technology that generates electricity from human motion, particularly when walking or running. Their flagship product is a shoe insole equipped with a small generator that captures the kinetic energy produced while walking and converts it into electrical power. This technology can be used to promote sustainability and provide practical solutions for powering small electronic devices while you walk. For example, residents and visitors could use SolePower's smart insoles to charge their smartphones or wearable devices while walking around town. This approach to energy harvesting reduces reliance on traditional power sources and encourages physical activity and outdoor exploration. The wearable technology has a broad range of applications beyond personal devices. It could be integrated into work boots for construction workers, hikers, or outdoor enthusiasts, providing a convenient and renewable power source for communication devices, safety equipment, or GPS trackers. By partnering with SolePower and embracing its wearable energy harvesting technology, Wellington could showcase its commitment to sustainability and innovation while empowering individuals to contribute to a greener future through everyday activities like walking. How about a partnership with the Wellington Walkers Are Welcome? These ideas could complement the numerous projects that already exist in the town and continue towards an electric future. This could complement projects by environmentally focussed Community Place Makers such as Wappenshall Junction Restoration, Friends of Apley Woods, Friends of Dothill Nature Reserve, The Peace Gardeners, and Friends of Wellington Station, who have all contributed to the development of green spaces for everyone to enjoy.

Here is what Electric Wellington might look like in the future:

Wellington market is open in the evenings, one day per week, and its lights are powered for those extra hours by electricity generated from sensors on its floor that people walk on during market days. The stalls are a patchwork of reclaimed materials, each one a testament to ingenuity and eco-friendly aesthetics. Here, the air is thick with the scents of fresh produce, baked bread, and artisanal cheeses, promising a simpler, better life with every bite. The food court is abundant with foods from around the world and the market remains at the heart of Wellington as it always has. Some of the buildings have developed vertical gardens, lush and green, making each structure a living, breathing part of the ecosystem. Rainwater harvesting systems capture the gentle rain from rooftops and store it for nurturing gardens and sustaining various town aspects. The market square has been fully refurbished, and any empty buildings have been sympathetically restored, with the owners playing their part and respecting the town's history and future. There are now more opportunities for people to live in central Wellington, and that has increased its sense of community and brought the spirit of the popular late-night market events into the town.

Electric Wellington is a place where the community isn't just a collection of individuals; it's a collection of entrepreneurs. There are festivals that turn the market square into a collection of colour and sound and workshops where knowledge about sustainable living is shared freely. It's a town that has managed to balance cutting-edge technology and nature's timeless rhythms. In Electric Wellington, you don't just live - you flourish. It's a living blueprint of how things could be if we all decided to be kinder to the planet and integrated it with existing technology. The town's achievements highlight the transformative potential of kindness and community-driven initiatives while also underscoring the enduring complexities of urban development. Wellington is an inspiring example of community resilience and collective action; it's a revival that embodies hope and realism.

Chapter Thirteen

International Wellington

Wellington has successfully reinvented itself and is on the road to revival, thanks to the collective efforts of the local council, business owners, and "Love Wellington." This has provided an opportunity for independent shops to flourish and add to the existing business landscape. Sally Themans continues to develop her love of towns and assist them in achieving their potential. In Wellington, she has succeeded in providing a platform for businesses and groups and the town is now in a stronger position than it has been in many years. With a level of success already achieved, it is time to build on this progress and cultivate more international connections to attract additional visitors to the town. Wellington has already acquired some international connections due to its twin town Chatenay-Malabry in France, which has been in place for more than 20 years thanks to the work of the Wellington and District Twinning Association, supported by the Wellington Council. There is already a list of exciting events that take place throughout the summer. However, there is room for autumn events that could help maintain interest in the town. An increase in international links is capable of providing an opportunity for unique events and an increase in visitor numbers. I am happy to provide ideas which might facilitate such activity and contribute towards the development of Wellington as a thriving market town.

Le Phun, a remarkable street theatre company from Toulouse, France, has captivated audiences worldwide with their unique performances. Their use of public spaces and recycled objects creates an experience that is truly one-of-a-kind. Their popular piece, "The Seedlings Revenge," unfolds over four days, immersing spectators in a world of dreams. Witnessing Le Phun's performances is an unforgettable experience as they breathe new life into the world of street theatre. International street theatre has the power to transport audiences to enchanting realms where imagination knows no bounds. In the hands of visionary directors, such productions can transform ordinary spaces into magical landscapes, inviting audiences on extraordinary journeys of wonder and discovery. Le Phun's innovative approach to theatre, characterized by immersive experiences and interactive storytelling, mirrors the transformative power of Shakespeare's enchanted forests or Prospero's mystical island. In a similar way, Le Phun's productions transport audiences into fantastical worlds where dreams come to life, encouraging those who observe to become involved in the story that they create.

Wellington's Market Square is perfectly positioned to host international events and remains the beating heart of such activities. Its central location and ample space make it an ideal venue for a diverse array of events that can captivate and draw in visitors from around the globe. The possibilities are endless, from cultural festivals and international sports tournaments to themed markets and innovative pop-up events. These events would complement existing local festivities that celebrate Wellington's rich heritage and culture, such as traditional food festivals showcasing local delicacies and music festivals featuring live performances from both local and international artists. The

Market Square has the potential to host innovative international events, such as silent discos under the stars and pop-up art installations, to create an immersive sensory experience. By embracing creativity and experimentation, Market Square can evolve into a dynamic space that consistently astonishes and pleases visitors, enhancing Wellington's reputation as a destination for unforgettable experiences. The square's ample space and central location make it capable of hosting a variety of international events that complement its existing activities, turning it into a hub for learning, personal growth, and increased international activity. For example, it could host a Mediterranean event promoting the Orange House Tapas Restaurant, featuring an authentic Spanish guitar recital and dancers. The Market Square could host a variety of events that engage visitors of all ages and showcase the best of Wellington. It could serve as a platform for local and international talent through performances, exhibitions, and cultural showcases, celebrating Wellington's creativity and historical heritage.

After navigating a series of challenging years, we must collectively take a deep breath and rediscover the joy of having fun. Life has been a whirlwind of uncertainties and pressures, making it more important than ever to carve out moments of happiness and light-heartedness. Whether it's a spontaneous weekend getaway, a lively dinner with friends, or simply indulging in your favourite hobbies, finding joy in the little things can do wonders for our well-being. Let's embrace laughter, relaxation, and connection, and remember that even amidst life's difficulties, we all deserve a chance to unwind and savour the good times. Now, more than ever, we should be glad to embrace the simple pleasures that we were deprived of for so long. Imagine the sheer delight of gathering with loved ones and friends, sharing laughter and stories that make the heart light. There's nothing quite like the joy of breathing fresh air during a morning walk, feeling the sun on your face, and appreciating the beauty of the world around you. Whether it's a heartfelt conversation over coffee or a spontaneous get-together, engaging with people reminds us of the irreplaceable value of human connection. Let's cherish the thrill of attending events, be it a lively concert, a local festival, or a casual community gathering, where the buzz of shared experiences brings a renewed sense of belonging. Relishing in your favourite hobbies, like reading a good book, gardening, or cooking a meal from scratch, can be incredibly fulfilling. These moments, no matter how small, remind us of the richness life has to offer. So, let's embrace laughter, relaxation, and connection. Remember that even amidst life's difficulties, we all deserve a chance to unwind and savour the good times. It's about finding joy in the little things, celebrating our resilience, and appreciating the renewed ability to live fully and freely once again.

Here are some ideas that could bring more visitors to Wellington this autumn:

Wellington's Got Talent: A talent show for local residents to showcase their skills in singing, dancing, comedy, and other performing arts. Prizes are awarded to the winners.

Wellness in Wellington: A weekend dedicated to promoting health and wellness. It features yoga sessions, nutrition workshops, mindfulness activities, and health screenings for the community.

Outdoor Cinema Night: Classic and contemporary films are screened under the stars, complete with popcorn stands and cosy seating arrangements for families and friends to enjoy a movie night out.

Tai Chi in the Square: Weekly sessions of Tai Chi in the town square offer residents a serene environment to practice this ancient Chinese martial art and promote physical and mental well-being.

The Prisoner Experience: An immersive event inspired by the cult classic TV series "The Prisoner." It features themed activities such as a giant chess game, interactive puzzles, and a display of vintage Caterham 7 cars reminiscent of the show's iconic vehicle.

Bowie Night: A tribute event honouring the music and legacy of David Bowie. It features live cover bands performing his greatest hits, themed costume contests, and art installations inspired by his iconic style and persona.

Opera in the Square: Enjoy a beautiful evening of operatic performances in the open-air setting of the town square. Local and guest singers will perform arias and duets from beloved operas, accompanied by live orchestral music.

Light Show: On this special evening, the upper floors of buildings surrounding the town square are illuminated, creating a magical ambience and offering a unique atmosphere.

Steampunk Extravaganza: A celebration of eccentric contraptions, elaborate costumes, and quirky performances inspired by the Victorian era's vision of futuristic technology. It features "Steam Powered Giraffe," a band with 16 million hits on YouTube with their song "Honeybee."

Interactive Light Maze: This installation is a labyrinth of glowing pathways with shifting colours. It challenges visitors to navigate through an ever-changing maze of light and shadow, offering a sensory exploration of space and perception.

Glow-in-the-Dark Carnival: Experience a neon-infused carnival with glowing rides, games, and attractions that come to life after dark. It transforms the town square into a psychedelic playground of light and colour.

Interdimensional Drum Circle: Join the communal drumming experience in the town square. Participants gather to create rhythmic patterns and harmonic vibrations that resonate across dimensions, fostering a sense of unity and connection beyond the boundaries of space and time.

Waltz Darling Wonderland: Immerse yourself in the enchanting world of Waltz, featuring a live performance of the iconic waltzes by a small orchestra and an invitation to dance the night away in the square.

Giant Football Tournament: This is a large-scale football (soccer) tournament played in the market square. Teams compete on an oversized inflatable field. Spectators can enjoy the action from surrounding cafes and stands set up around the square.

Urban Harmonics: A group of musicians forms a circle outside the town and, at an agreed-upon time, begins to walk towards the market square while playing their instruments to a prearranged set of chords. This concept is based on the "Urban Sax" concept developed in Paris.

Wassail Celebration: This traditional celebration is held in the Market Square. Attendees can participate in the ancient ritual of blessing the apple orchards for a bountiful harvest, accompanied by singing, dancing, and mulled cider.

Mummer's Play Performance: The Market Square celebrates a centuries-old theatrical tradition with a traditional mummer's play featuring local actors, colourful costumes, comedic antics, and audience participation.

Mermaid Festival: This festival celebrates the mythical mermaids said to inhabit the waters of Shropshire's rivers and lakes. It features mermaid-themed performances, storytelling sessions, and art installations in the Market Square.

After enduring a string of serious and challenging years, it's time we all take a collective deep breath and rediscover the joy of having fun. Life has been a whirlwind of uncertainties and pressures, making it more important than ever to carve out moments of happiness and light-heartedness. Now, more than ever, we should be glad and treasure the simple pleasures that we were deprived of for so long. Just picture the pure joy of gathering with loved ones and friends, sharing laughter and stories that warm the heart. There's truly nothing like the happiness of breathing in fresh air during a morning walk, feeling the sun on your face, and admiring the beauty of the world around you. Interacting with people, whether it's having a heartfelt conversation over coffee or joining a spontaneous get-together, reminds us of the irreplaceable value of human connection. Let's appreciate the excitement of attending events, like a lively concert, a local festival, or a casual community gathering, where the shared experiences bring a renewed sense of belonging. Enjoying your favourite hobbies, such as reading a good book, gardening, or cooking a meal from scratch, can be incredibly fulfilling. These moments, no matter how small, remind us of the richness life has to offer.

In imagining the revitalization of Wellington's streets, the addition of vibrant street theatre provides a compelling avenue for cultural enrichment and community engagement. Just imagine the lively streets adorned with diverse performances, captivating both local residents and visitors. By hiring a variety of street theatre companies, Wellington could transform its public spaces into dynamic stages, fostering a lively atmosphere that celebrates creativity and diversity. One example of an international street theatre company is Royal de Luxe, based in France. Renowned for its awe-inspiring giant marionettes and immersive performances, Royal de Luxe has mesmerized audiences worldwide with its imaginative storytelling and larger-than-life productions. Another notable company is Grupo Puja!, hailing from Spain, known for its innovative street theatre performances that blend physical theatre, circus arts, and interactive storytelling to create unforgettable experiences. Closer to home, Wellington could also engage local street theatre companies such as The Loons Circus Theatre Company, recognized for their inventive blend of circus skills, comedy, and audience participation. Additionally, Te Rākau Theatre, with its unique approach to Indigenous storytelling and community-based performances, would bring a distinctively Kiwi flavour to Wellington's streets. So, let's embrace laughter, relaxation, and connection. Remember that even amidst life's difficulties, we all deserve a chance to decompress and experience good times. It's about finding joy in the little things, celebrating our resilience, and appreciating the renewed ability to live fully and freely once again.

Chapter Fourteen

Four hours to save Wellington!

During my research for this book, I found myself in a situation that many of us can relate to - I received a parking fine. This happened because I overstayed at a private car park in Wellington. Having recently moved back from Manchester, I wasn't as familiar with Wellington's parking regulations as I used to be. I mistakenly assumed that the car park was inactive, leading to my oversight. Since then, I have revisited Wellington multiple times, conducted some excellent interviews, and reacquainted myself with the town. To be fair, the company managing the car park was just doing their job. Now that I'm aware of the time limit, I can't help but wonder why the limit was only two hours? It doesn't seem long enough to explore a town that has so much to offer. What about the needs of disabled or elderly visitors? Or young families with children and pushchairs? After learning my lesson, I opted for a council-run car park on subsequent visits to see if it would be an improvement. I had to walk further, and the time limit was always at the back of my mind during these visits. I really needed more time to enjoy Wellington in an equitable way, and four hours of parking would have been great!

The influence of parking times on customer behaviour in a market town is a crucial aspect that should not be overlooked. It affects shopping patterns and has a profound impact on the area's economic vitality. When parking times are limited, customers tend to make quick trips, focusing on specific purchases and neglecting to explore or enjoy additional amenities. This can result in reduced spending in local shops and eateries as customers rush to avoid parking penalties. On the other hand, longer parking times encourage leisurely visits, allowing shoppers to explore more stores and contribute more to the local economy. Real-world examples from Altrincham, Cheshire, and Sudbury, Suffolk, demonstrate this. In these towns, increasing parking times led to a noticeable increase in foot traffic and retail sales. Customers felt less pressured and more inclined to explore the town, boosting the local economy. These examples underscore the potential of adjusting parking regulations to create a more inviting shopping environment, thereby fostering economic growth through an enhanced customer experience.

In Copenhagen, Denmark, the city of Frederiksberg extended parking times from two to four hours, positively impacting customer behaviour and the local economy. This policy change aimed to encourage more visitors to spend time in the area, exploring its shops, cafes, and cultural attractions without the pressure of rushing back to their cars. The result was a substantial increase in foot traffic and retail activity. Local businesses reported higher sales and the extended parking time allowed customers to combine shopping with dining and other leisure activities. This success in Frederiksberg demonstrates the potential for other European cities to adopt similar strategies to boost their local economies, highlighting the importance of thoughtful parking policies in enhancing the overall visitor experience and stimulating economic growth. From a legal perspective, laws such as the Equality Act 2010, the Blue Badge Scheme, and the Public Sector Equality Duty require *reasonable adjustments* to ensure that disabled individuals are not disadvantaged. Insufficient parking times can hinder compliance with these laws by not allowing people with mobility issues enough time to complete their tasks, potentially leading to breaches. Additionally, the Traffic Management Act 2004 and the Chronically Sick and Disabled Persons Act 1970 mandate local authorities to provide adequate parking facilities for disabled individuals. Thus, restrictive parking durations can disproportionately affect disabled individuals, undermining legal protections and accessibility provisions. For this reason and many more, free parking for four hours in all car parks in Wellington would be a game changer for the town and allow both young and old to enjoy spending time in the town. Let's imagine how this might look like by following a fictional group of visitors to Wellington when free four-hour parking has been established:

In the heart of Wellington, a bustling market town with a friendly atmosphere, a group of elderly friends reunite for their weekly outings. As they slowly make their way through the town, each step carefully taken, they can't help but notice the newfound sense of freedom granted by the extended parking times. Their mobility had been limited for years, confined to quick visits and rushed errands due to strict parking regulations. At times, they even skipped visits to the town, with some friends opting to visit Telford Town Centre instead. However, today is different. With four hours at their disposal, they savour each moment, taking their time to explore the independent shops and cafes before going for lunch at the Orange House Mediterranean Restaurant, where there is a Spanish guitar recital. Margaret, one of the group, leans on her trusty walking cane and pauses to look at the window of The Little Pantry while her friend Ron examines the guitars in the Guitar Vault. Meanwhile, with a gentle smile etched on his face,

John finds himself drawn to the Gratitude Café, where he hears Dave serenading his customers while Michelle looks after them. Sylvia and Harold, arm in arm, find themselves in the Gaming Café and enjoy playing "Kerplunk" with one of its owners while having a coffee and sharing tales of days gone by. They all agree to meet at the Orbit Cinema to watch "The Power of Love" by The Andre Rieu Orchestra but realize they have got the wrong day and stay to watch "Catching Fire: The Story of Anita Pallenberg" instead!

Meanwhile, Sarah and Tom, parents to adventurous twins Sophie and Max, enjoy the freedom afforded by the new parking times. With plenty of time to spare, they embark on a journey of discovery, wandering through the town and market, finding lots of things to buy. Their children's imaginations run wild as they pretend to be pirates searching for hidden treasure. Their laughter rings out as they scour every nook and cranny in search of adventure and end up at the "Book Ends Bookshop", where they are greeted warmly by its owners. As the sun begins to set, families gather in the market square, the air alive with the sound of chatter and laughter. Children run freely, their faces flushed with the thrill of exploration, while parents watch on with pride and joy. As they make their way back to their parked cars, with shopping and memories made, they appreciate the precious moments of togetherness that the extended parking hours have granted them in the heart of Wellington. The parents experience less stress because they have more time, and the children are happier as they can play with other children for longer. A few hours make a big difference!

In a span of four hours, which amounts to 240 minutes, you can embark on countless adventures. Just imagine diving into a gripping novel, getting lost in its pages as the minutes tick by, or creating a culinary masterpiece while experimenting with flavours and textures. You might go for a long, leisurely walk, allowing your mind to wander and appreciate the world around you. Perhaps you could spend the time binge-watching your favourite TV series, with each episode unfolding like a chapter in an epic saga, or immersing yourself in a video game, becoming a hero in a virtual world. If you're inclined towards creativity, you could write several pages of your own novel or paint a new piece of art. Musicians might compose a new song, capturing the essence of their emotions in melodies and harmonies. Or you could use the time for self-care, indulging in a spa-like experience at home, meditating, or practising yoga to centre your mind and body. According to the philosopher Seneca, who pondered deeply on the nature of time, "It's not that we have little time, but more that we waste a good deal of it." In 240 minutes, you could learn a new skill, reconnect with an old friend, or simply sit quietly and contemplate each moment's richness. We can also choose to spend those 240 minutes shopping in Wellington and enjoying established and independent businesses. It's just an idea, but if the Council and the private parking company make a *reasonable adjustment*, they could do the town a tremendous favour and boose the economy of the town, especially when it has done so well in the last few years. Wellington could be saved from losing valuable customers and increase its inclusivity in the bargain! And all it would take is four hours!

Chapter Fifteen
Conclusion

Wellington is experiencing a revival resulting from a combined effort by several individuals and organisations. Individuals such as Sally and Paula from 'Love Wellington,' Mark the Barber, Les the Cobbler, Mark from Telford Angling, Lisa the Cheese Lady, Jon from the Gaming Café, Jake from the Guitar Shop, Kelli from the Little Pantry, Ray and Damien from The Orbit Cinema, Rob from H2A, and Anthony from Anthony's Farm Shop and Café and many more, have each played a crucial role. Their collective efforts, along with the support of the council and government funding, have built a strong community, supported local businesses, and helped to preserve Wellington's heritage. As they continue to collaborate and innovate, guided by a shared vision of revival, the future of Wellington is filled with promise. Their collective endeavours ensure that Wellington is not just a place on the map but a dynamic community that embodies the essence of small-town charm and resilience.

Mark's Barbers is not just a barbershop; it's a hub where locals share their life stories and forge connections. Les the Cobbler's shoe repair shop is a problem-solving hub where things are fixed. Mark from Telford Angling brings the joy of relaxation and fishing to Wellington, while Lisa, the Cheese Lady, introduces residents to a world of artisanal cheeses. Jon at the Gaming Café presides over a haven for gamers, a place where friendships and community bonds are nurtured over shared interests. Jake from the Guitar Shop provides quality instruments and fuels the dreams of budding musicians. Kelli's Little Pantry has introduced a new way of shopping, and Ray and Damien from

The Orbit Cinema create magical experiences on the silver screen and provide a community hub for groups and events. Anthony's Farm Shop and Café celebrates the bounty of the land, offering fresh produce and homemade treats. Rob from H2A continues to organise historical events in the town, encouraging improved shop fronts and a consistent palate of colour that brings a sense of joy and colour to the town. This is complemented by the work of Sally and her assistant Paola from "Love Wellington", who have brought all these things together. Let's not forget the contributions made by Councillor Anthony Lowe and his colleagues, as well as the Californian vibe created by Dave and Michelle at the Gratitude Café and raise a glass to brothers Steve and Peter at the award-winning Pheasant Inn, Rowton Brewery, and Wrekin Pub. You can add to that a host of busy volunteer groups that each contribute to the well-being of Wellington. These combined efforts represent the heartbeat of Wellington's revival and embody the town's resilience, independence and unwavering spirit. They provide essential services and entertainment, cater to diverse interests and hobbies, and foster a sense of belonging and engagement among residents. Collectively, they form a dynamic ecosystem that drives economic growth and social cohesion and preserves the character and heritage of Wellington. They inspire hope and optimism, laying the foundation for generations to come to thrive in a vibrant and resilient community.

Wellington still retains some of its architectural heritage, and it is great to see some of its buildings being sympathetically restored. While the town has lost some of its architectural structures over the years, recent efforts have been made to preserve and revitalize the remaining treasures. The town aims to honour its past while looking towards the future by refreshing exteriors and revitalizing interiors. One of the key aspects of Wellington's future is its market square, which can attract a large number of visitors on a regular basis. These visitors can then enjoy exploring the various independent shops that have been encouraged to flourish in the town. The small businesses that have emerged in the town offer a unique charm and character that cannot be replicated by chain stores. The eclectic mix of independent businesses, cafes, and artisanal shops that dot the town contribute immensely to its revitalized identity and charm. Independent shops play a crucial role in providing a platform for local entrepreneurs to showcase their talents and creativity. By supporting these small businesses, Wellington is able to introduce a sense of authenticity and individuality into its commercial landscape, adding to the town's appeal and creating a unique shopping experience.

Some argue that larger businesses hold the key to unlocking job opportunities and driving economic growth within a town. They point to the potential limitations faced by independent businesses, such as their comparatively limited resources for marketing and advertising. Moreover, there is concern about the sustainability of independent ventures in the long run, particularly in the face of fierce competition and fluctuating economic conditions. These arguments underscore the challenges that independent businesses encounter while competing with larger corporations, raising questions about their viability and resilience in today's competitive market landscape. There are also those who think that staying in one's comfort zone provides a sense of security that is more important than the thrill of new adventures. While it's true that staying within our comfort zones can offer a sense of security, let's not forget the magic that can sometimes await beyond its borders.

Despite facing increased competition and economic uncertainties, Wellington's independent businesses have persevered and demonstrated their unwavering commitment to serving the local community. They have emerged stronger than ever by embracing innovative strategies and leveraging their unique charm. However, it is important to recognize that success can sometimes breed complacency. Therefore, prudent management and thoughtful planning are paramount to preserve the town's unique character and identity while fostering continued growth and prosperity. Wellington's independent businesses have proven their resilience in the face of adversity, emerging as pillars of strength for the town's economy Their ability to respond to changing circumstances has sustained the local economy and reaffirmed the town's vibrant community spirit. By prioritizing the continued success of independent businesses, Wellington can ensure that the town remains a dynamic hub of activity and discovery for generations to come. The success of independent businesses in Wellington goes beyond economic prosperity. These businesses are more than just places to shop; they are also community gathering spots where people come together to exchange ideas, make memories, and form lasting friendships.

As Wellington navigates its way through the aftermath of the pandemic and the impact of out-of-town developments, the resilience of its independent businesses serves as a beacon of hope and inspiration. These small enterprises have weathered the storm and become integral pillars of the community, forging strong bonds with residents and visitors alike. However, as the town experiences a resurgence in economic activity and renewed interest from investors, it faces a pivotal moment in its development. Town leaders and stakeholders must approach growth with caution and foresight, prioritizing long-term sustainability over short-term gains. By nurturing and supporting the growth of independent businesses while safeguarding the town's heritage and character, Wellington can ensure a bright and prosperous future for generations to come. In conclusion, the success of Wellingtonia's independent businesses is a testament to the town's creativity, resilience, and community spirit. By supporting these businesses, Wellington can continue to thrive as a unique and authentic destination, offering its residents and visitors a glimpse into the heart and soul of the town.

To conclude this section of the book I am going to include two comments which have resonated with me as I researched this book. While shopping at Anthony's of Wellington, I was introduced to local author David Weston…who had this to say:

"Wellington has reached the point where it can stop looking inwards and start to look outwards internationally."

This is a good point and one that supports some of the comments presented in this book. I am going to leave the last word to Ray Hughes, a respected director at Wellington Orbit Cinema, whose thoughtful determination continues to represent a driving force behind Wellington's revival:

"I think the thing for Wellington is you've got to look forward; you can't use the past as a recipe for the future".

Well said, sir…I couldn't agree more!

Part Two

Interviews with business owners and those involved with Wellington's revival

Chapter One

Sally Themans

Director

There are two ladies of Wellington fame

Who bring love and respect to that name

Like a beacon of light

They do what is right

And continue to promote that refrain

Can you let me know your name and role in Wellington?

"My name is Sally Themans, and I'm the Director of "Love Wellington". I have been hired to provide a platform for Wellington businesses and to promote the town. This has included a website and a magazine".

It has been interesting looking through the previous editions of the "Wellington Magazine" to see how you kept adding things every month until you reached where you are now.

"It's quite funny because when I was looking for the link for you, I went down a rabbit hole and started looking at old editions, and it was Mike and I's ideas in 2019 to produce a magazine and little did I know that sixteen editions later that it would be the same thing! And the other person to talk to, and he is quite a political figure, is Lee Carter. He is a town and borough councillor. He has also been instrumental in the regeneration group and very much from the Telford and Wrekin point of view behind the grants and some of those initiatives, and they have really helped to stimulate investment".

I want to celebrate all the hard work that has gone into creating a positive moment in Wellington's history.

"One of the first businesses to open in the new era was a restaurant called "The Walnut" which is gone now...everything runs its course. That was the first quality food offer and from that, I am just trying to think of who came next. It was probably Park Street Kitchen when they started doing that development in the market. I love the term "flocking" that you have mentioned before because when one or two came, they all wanted to come, and a big win for Wellington is the Red Brick Café, which is run by Zack Hammond, who is a proven operator from Shrewsbury. From my perspective, his decision to come to Wellington was just "wow" he could really make a difference".

Were you surprised by the success of the late-night market?

"I was there for the first one, and I couldn't believe how many people were there, and it was really interesting…my daughter, who was at Exeter University at the time, and she was coming home, and I suggested that she catch the train from Birmingham to Wolverhampton and meet me in Wellington? She is a drama student, super trendy, and quite a foodie, and she just wandered around that market and just said, "I can't believe this is Wellington…this feels like Exeter or Bristol!" I know that quite a few people came from Shifnal, and I targeted it hard using Facebook ads in Shrewsbury and Wolverhampton. However, when you look around most of those people are from Wellington. They are Wellington People who never had a place…who always went to Birmingham, go to Digbeth Dinner's Club, go to the late-night market in Shrewsbury, and actually the delight that they expressed at having their own answer to those places on their doorstep was terrific, and it's really important that we build on that and keep them coming"

When did you begin working on the idea of "Love Wellington"

"They approached me in 2018 to come and work there, and I did a lot of research before I arrived. I had already been working on "Love Bridgenorth", and that had been successful, and we had won the "high street award". Wellington was such a different animal, and how it was trading at the time was very much a secondary place...hairdressers and opticians and very little to retail to draw people in. But when you look at the demographics, Wellington is such a lovely old town, and there is a lot of wealth on the outside, but the inside is very poor and at heel. There was poor housing and poor business, and all those people who would send their children to Wrekin College would jump into their cars or jump on the train and head straight to Shrewsbury. They would not countenance going into Wellington unless they were going to get their eyes tested or something like that or go for a haircut. It was the Mayor of Wellington in about 2022 who made a comment to me, and I didn't hide the fact that I was trying to pull in the wealthier residents, and I talked about getting them to rediscover Wellington. If they had decided to stay living there, then surely, they wanted it to be good. I just remember him saying after I started working on the project..."I have noticed that people just seem better dressed - the people coming into the cafes are slightly better healed"

I can testify to this as well. I was inspired to write this book because I came into town one day and noticed a couple in matching camel coats who were dressed so elegantly, like people used to be when they came into town.

"In a way, it's a case of re-emergence. My mother-in-law was born in Wellington and she was born on Haygate farm, which is a lovely old building and was, until recently, the Orlaton restaurant; it's the building by the monkey puzzle tree. That's where she was born, and she was part of a big farming family. My mother-in-law would always wear white gloves whenever she went to Wellington…it was the poshest place in Shropshire, but it lost its way. I wrote some on LinkedIn the other day about reimaging and repurposing vacant places in the high street. On the 22nd of October, I organised a conference in the Shrewsbury Museum, and we had someone called O.J. MacDonald speaking. He was the keynote speaker, and he was the CEO of something like the Institute of Town Managers, and he is "Mr Highstreet". Anyway, he came up to Shrewsbury to speak, and the theme was re-purposing empty spaces on the high street, and we had a couple of case studies, and one of them was "The Orbit", and Andy Smith came and spoke, and we had a place in Bridgenorth which we had re-purposed".

What made you decide to follow this particular direction in your career?

"I started something called "Love Bridgenorth" in 2015, and I was amazed at the reception, and the response that it got, and people loved it...they loved being reminded how nice their town is, and I used something called the "Genius Loci". It's great when you go to a conference, and you think "Oh Gosh he is talking about something I have been doing instinctively. It's really about when you are talking about a place and promoting a place and focussing on three things...the first thing being the history and the reason behind a place and why it came to be there, and people love who lived there and what did they do there as well as more recent history. The more physical attributes are also important; it's not an accident that every three or four weeks, I will upload a picture of the Wrekin onto the Wellington Facebook page, or I will take a picture of some of the lovely Georgian buildings in Wellington. So again, the physical presence and that are all bound together by the people's sentiments, how they actually feel and how they are connected to a place. So, when I am planning what is going to go into "Our Wellington" and what is going to go out in social media messages, it's very much with that behind it. It's not just random...I am random if things are going on, and I can react and embrace those aspects, and that's what's going on when I am promoting Wellington. I also have a marketing calendar, and it's just straightforward marketing. I did a marketing degree, and I work with businesses and its "It's Shrove Tuesday...what can we do around that?" It's

midsummer...that's why I love the things that Rob Francis does on Charter Day. That encompasses an event and the history of Wellington. There are certain points in the diary, and either the town council will organise events or will at least do some sort of promotional activity around those. At half-term Halloween time, we will have a pumpkin trail, and at Easter time, we will have an Easter trail, and those are all the things that drive footfall into the town".

"Therefore, we have a list of things we can do to promote the town, and it is underlaid all the time with those aspects, which is great and then good news stories appear like somebody's got a grant or there's a new owner...I can't control those, but they are the things that's that I will point out to people. There is also, and this is where my marketing comes in and there is also a voice and a brand, and I have brand guidelines. By that, I mean the Brand and what the brand must say and mustn't say. It's one step removed from the council, and I don't want to come across as being part of the council...when I first told the council, who are my paymasters, that I thought it was important to be separate, they were a bit grumpy and said, "But we want people to know that we are investing in you!" However, it is a fact that people are always ready to slate the council for one reason or another and every time I went into the market, someone would start complaining about not getting their bins empty or something like that! So, I said it's got to be separate, so it is just about the positives. I think that

if you said to say to people in Wellington if they have heard of "Love Wellington", then hopefully, they would say yes!"

"If you asked people how they think that it is funded, most people would scratch their heads and say "no". I don't make any secret of the fact that it is funded by the council, but certainly, at the beginning, it was kept at arms distance. I have also tried to tell them that the council need to have a different voice because they have a different function to "Love Wellington". You know, the council is there to make sure that everything is compliant, to make sure that streets are cleaned, and hopefully, we have taken that a step further to include that businesses are supported because most councils don't go that far. It's not the council's job to say, "Let's have a Valentine's Day event" or "Wow, doesn't this window look lovely". I don't think that the council should do that, and I think that "Love Wellington" has been much more frivolous and enthusiastic. I spend a lot of time curating photographs to make them inviting…it's marketing, it's PR".

"The Council have done amazing things, and they have the funding to make things happen and "Love Wellington" and the Council are independent. They came along to get things started with people like Keli King at The Little Green Pantry and Jake at the Music Shop, but they can't just throw money at things. You have to do it with lots of genuine PR and Marketing. And yes, the Council can write press releases, but it uses that constantly engage with them as says, "Look at this…look at Jake and his guitars". So, I would liken it to the

Council can do the big things like buying the market, which they have just done and sweeping up and making sure that the community is coming along with them, so they are really independent and should be complimentary".

Can you tell me about the pandemic and how the town managed this situation?

"Because things were in place and because we were already connected on WhatsApp group because I had already set that up...it was much easier to keep in touch with all the businesses and communicate with them and what was going on and get their views and opinions on when we could get things going again and how they wanted to do that. We had several online meetings, and the retailers all came to those. We did some welcome back to Wellington stickers on the pavement and some banners. We also did a "Please remember to wear your facemask" promotion, and one of the businesses sponsored it and did the design work. And so, there was quite a good sense of camaraderie which would not have happened earlier. They were all able to get to know each other and support each other. Kelli from the Little Pantry and Tony from Anthony's Butchers did deliveries, and lots of them did. We created a living online directory of who was open and what they were doing and keeping that as current as possible. The things we could do we did and things like the "lights switch on" in 2020 were virtual. we also did a VE Day celebration in 2020 in the lockdown, and we managed to get BBC Midlands today to attend today. People were having virtual street parties and things like that.

They came along because SKY News was interested, and I had organised a list of events. Then SKY pulled out the day before, so I contacted BBC Midlands on Twitter and said, "This is what we have planned for Wellington...this is what we have planned. Do you want to join us?" So, at seven in the morning, I nearly didn't see the message. I was just getting ready and about to have a shower before heading to Wellington, and the message said, "Yes, we are changing everything around, and we will be with you at ten o'clock. That was a brilliant thing for Wellington, and VE Day was centred on Wellington".

Where do you think you have got up to now with "Love Wellington"

"I am very proud...I am really proud of what has been achieved and when they first asked me, I was really unsure, but what we have done with "Good to Great" is that other towns have asked me, and I am working with Shifnal Town Council and have worked with Madley Town Council. What we have done now is identify what works and create a process, and it is now tried and tested. It has worked really well in four places. I am proud of that, and I think there is more to do in Wellington; there is going to be a change in personnel because Paola is leaving us, and she has been with me during the whole project and played an important role. I look forward to continuing my role with "Love Wellington" I have been working on it for four years and just hope that people can see the benefits".

How would you like to see "Love Wellington" develop in the future?

"I think we need to keep on with it; we have had a few openings and closings of businesses. We are not out of the water yet, and then we have the cost-of-living crisis, which doesn't really help, and people have less money in their pockets. But what I also want to see is some long-term changes in behaviour. I don't know about you, but now that I am shopping for two instead of five as my children have flown the nest, I am now using the refill shops, I use the local baker, the local butcher, and I am thinking about my great supermarket shops and…it's now tiny supermarket shops. The things that I can't get in my high street, and that's what I advocate all the time, and it's nice to be doing it and seeing that it can work…so I hope that we can change people's long-term behaviour".

Chapter Two

Paola Armstrong
Administrator

In an office where tasks often fray,

An administrator leads us each day.

With skill so refined,

And a sharp, clever mind,

New Zealand is now where she'll play

Can you give me your name and your professional role:

"I am Paola Armstrong. I work for Wellington Town Council, and half of my role is to plan and run the events as well as the communications, while the other half is working for "Love Wellington", which promotes the town and its positive aspects. Furthermore, this has escalated and snowballed quite a lot since I have joined, and we now work with businesses and the community groups and pull things together and do campaign trails and try and encourage footfall in the town".

I have noticed a positive change in the town, with many new and established businesses. How long has this been going on, and who has contributed to this success?

"Love Wellington" has been going on for four years, and it was the brainchild of Sally Themans, who lives in Bridgenorth and set up "Love Bridgenorth" on a voluntary basis. Sally is a high street expert, and the thing she did in Bridgenorth worked…it worked. It was all about getting the businesses together and bringing the communities together and promoting the best aspects of that town. So, thankfully for us, Wellington employed her as an external consultant. I think that was about a year or six months to a year before I joined and then my role was to kind of help her. We had met before, and it was just a dream job for me, really, and she let me go and do my thing, which was great".

It's the best thing you can do sometimes…trust people and let them do their thing.

"Yes, that's true".

You then had the pandemic to deal with; how did Love Wellington cope with that?

"It was a real challenge, as you can imagine. I had just started the job, and we didn't know what we were doing as we didn't have the premises or the council offices. So, it became obvious early on that it was about keeping people in touch and letting residents know who was open and as it slowly unfolded, businesses were very adaptable, and a lot of the hospitality businesses were doing takeaway and delivery services, and it was all about that…letting people know that Wellington is still here. We also did some filming and campaigns to show people that some businesses were still open. We promoted the idea of shopping local, and we put stickers on the floor. I went around with my son wearing masks and showed people about the hand sanitisers and informed them about the distancing rules that were in place".

Was there a particular low point during the pandemic for Wellington?

"We didn't really have time to think about it…I would describe Sally Themans as a forward thinker and a visionary, which was a great help during that serious time. We also have a few key people in Wellington, and it was just a way to get these

people together and decide what we could do because the businesses were going to really struggle under these circumstances. One thing that happened was that they set up a "click and collect" thing in the market and so businesses got together, and somebody could go in and collected the things. We didn't have it then, but perhaps as a result, we now have a cycle delivery service, and they are amazing. Wellington Town Council has now invested in an electric bike, and we have about sixteen volunteers who deliver for free".

What is the radius of this service?

"Well, it started in and around Wellington, and they have recently gone as far as Trench; it all depends on the cyclist and who is available. It would have been good in the pandemic, but there may well have been something positive to have emerged from that situation. There are about twenty to thirty thousand people in the Wellington area, and we have some elderly people who benefit from this service. It's a great scheme, and it's been going for just about a year and it's those kind of things that set us apart as a town".

So, it was creative thinking that solved the problem...

"Yes, definitely".

"Wellington market played an important role, and all the businesses pulled together really, which was great to see. Another example would be Anthonys the Butcher, who did an awful lot for their customers and delivered during this time as well. They have expanded and sold all sorts of things, with a focus on Shropshire produce. He has a great team and is very kind and looks after his customers, and now, a few years later, they will remember that and remain loyal".

What other campaigns did "Love Wellington" organise?

"Well, we did "Shop Local this Christmas" to try and encourage people to come in, and Kelli at the "Little Pantry" put together a video to "All I want for Christmas" by Maria Carey and asked us what we thought. We liked it and put it on the "Love Wellington" WhatsApp group. We then asked anyone who wanted to be involved, and she put it all together. This was just a way to promote shopping in Wellington, and in a few minutes, lots of people said they would like to participate. It was just a bit of fun at Christmas, but it does show how supportive the people in the business community are. Then we had the Wrekin rowers, the four chaps who rowed the Atlantic a couple of years ago. Two of them were from Wellington and one of them was a manager from Specsavers. We did an event in the square, and they bought their boat into the square just before they left for some promotion and fundraising. They then went off, I think it was in 2022, and they started the race, and I think it took about forty days, and all of Wellington got this tracking app and could see where they were. They had a Marlin strike, and it hit the boat underneath; it was all a big drama; they were deflated but had to keep going".

Can you let me know what happened next?

"Anthony Nichols, that is "Anthony's of Wellington", and a few others had this idea, and we got everybody in the square to sing this song that one of the chaps had written, and we all got in the square, and one of the partners of one of the men in the boat called them, and they heard it live in the Atlantic. So, afterwards, they said that it really gave them a lift to crack on and finish the race. The Marlin is a big fish, as you know, and it did a lot of damage, but two of the crew are builders, and they were able to fix the damage with a pack lunch box and some other things…and they did it. They finished the race. They did it for three charities, but unfortunately, one of the crew also found out that he had a serious illness and passed away. His funeral was in the town at All Saints, and it was jam-packed, it was a real inspirational funeral and everyone that left just thought what an amazing person he was and how lucky we were to have had him in our town. All of the Wrekin Rowers were taken in the hearts of the people in Wellington, and I think three of them came round and went around the businesses and thanked them and the green … which is our second refill shop, they did a raffle, and all of the stalls in the market donated prizes which was lovely. That was absolutely lovely, the way that everyone did that".

I understand you are relocating to New Zealand with your family in a few weeks. Several businesses are grateful for your hard work and dedication to Wellington Council and "Love Wellington."

"They are very kind... you get back what you put in definitely. I live here, and my children go to school, and my husband is from Wellington. My parents came to live here, and I love the town, but when I started this job, you have to go around and talk to people, and you are not in a rush, and you have the time to listen to what they're saying. You then realise that this town is not made up of businesses; it's made up of people! And when you can bring people together, things like "love Wellington" and you have events like today with the pancake race and the High Sheriff and the councillor. It's the way you can bring people closer and closer and bring the pieces of the jigsaw together...that's really important".

"I am definitely sad to leave, really sad to leave. We have built up a great community here, and I hope I've been a part of that. I think that it's going to continue to grow, and it will be interesting to see how it will grow from the other side of the world. We have social media now, and we do lots of live streams, so I will be able to watch from afar".

What would you like to see his part of your legacy?

"I think to just continue what it's doing, and they spent a lot of investment from the Telford and Wrekin, the Borough Council. We have been working with them, and they have been fantastic. They have really taken Wellington, and there is going to be a lot of investment here. They have bought the market as well, and there are going to be big changes in the Orbit Cinema. It is lovely to have seen the beginnings of it, and I look forward to coming back and visiting to see how it's all going. I think that it's all about balance, and what it needs is new stuff and old stuff, and I think that that will be the key to its success!"

Chapter Three

The Wellington Cobbler

There once was a cobbler so wise,

Crafting shoes with a gleam in his eyes.

In his workshop of leather,

he sold keys and umbrellas

and his efforts were regularly prized

Can you let me know your name and the name of your business?

"My name is Leslie Gough, and I am the Wellington cobbler!"

I understand you are the only key cutter in the village…is that correct?

"Absolutely! I'm the go-to guy for all your key-cutting needs and locksmith emergencies. I do shoe repairs, I do keep cutting, I do engravings bag repairs, and I sell shoe care equipment… Anything and everything. I was in the market for 15 years and have been here for 7 years. In 3 years', time, I would have been a cobbler for 50 years! I left school with no sort of grades or anything… then I saw an advert saying "training shoe repairer,… and I went in and got the job. For the 1st six months, I was sweeping, polishing and making tea, and then I was watching people as they were repairing. My job involves various things, and I have been self-employed for about 20 years. Why did Wellington survive the doughnut effect? Well, I think that Wellington is the traditional market town with proper people who like visiting the town… and there are lots of Wellington people who don't like visiting what I call the big green on the outer M 54 or as people call it the Telford centre. A lot of local people don't like using that, and that's why they like the tradition of old market towns".

Have you noticed any improvements in Wellington in the last few years?

"The doughnut effect does have an effect on some towns, and the younger folk like going up there because there are more high-class shops. At the moment, there isn't a lot for them in Wellington, apart from the market… there's nowhere where you can get a pair of shoes or ladies' outfitters, and that's a little bit sad…that's why we need that sort of thing. But the thing about the Wellington people is that they're really friendly, and they will give you a chance. "Love Wellington" is doing their best to regenerate the town, and they've made the market in the town better. They will come and chat, too, and tell you what's going on. They're trying their best. Another place that's been very positive is the Orbit cinema… they do a lot at the Orbit. After the pandemic, it seemed as if people wanted to be out and about and to be with each other again and experience shopping in town and fresh air! It suddenly became busier, and the families were out. After the first wave of the pandemic, when I came back, "Central News" was in town, and they interviewed me. It was almost like coming back and starting a new business. Everything was so different, and it was like starting again, and we soon got back into the swing of things. Then we had another wave and another wave, but it's coming along".

"I'll tell you one funny story: easter work for one of the big companies, and I was working one day on a Sunday actually, and this lady came in, and she said, "Can you help me?" and I

said, "Why what's the matter and she said, "My bra Strap's broke", and I was only a teenager then, and I was shaking and thinking what do I do? She said can you fix it for me, and I said "OK". Well, at that time, we had a little room round the back, and I said, OK, if you take it off, then I'll stitch it. So, the customer took it off, and I was nervous, as you can imagine. I turned the right way round and stitched it, and she put it back on. Happy days! And it didn't charge her. I didn't look either!"

You exhibited a professional attitude from an early age!

"If was older, I might have asked for her number" (Laughter)

Have there been any more humorous episodes?

"Well, it's funny how many people come into the shop and ask me if I cut keys, and I say no, that's just my wallpaper!"

What is the range of services you offer?

"Shoe repairs, key cutting, engraving, and bag repairs are integral to the skilled services offered by craftsmen who have honed their expertise over the years. In the world of shoe repairs, artisans showcase their mastery in preserving the longevity of beloved footwear, breathing new life into worn-out soles and weathered leather. It's not merely about mending a shoe but about the meticulous restoration that goes beyond the visible, preserving the essence and comfort of well-worn pairs. The art of key cutting is a testament to precision and security. With their deft hands, key cutters transform blanks into perfectly shaped

keys, ensuring the seamless function of locks and safeguarding cherished spaces. Engraving, on the other hand, elevates personalization to an art form. Whether inscribing names on trophies, engraving sentimental messages on jewellery, or immortalizing special moments on plaques, engravers infuse inanimate objects with profound meaning. Bag repairs encapsulate a blend of craftsmanship and functionality, where skilled hands stitch, patch, and refurbish bags to extend their utility and preserve their aesthetic appeal. Collectively, these services embody the artistry of tradespeople who not only fix tangible items but also contribute to the narrative of personal belongings, adding layers of character, memories, and individuality to the objects we interact with daily. As custodians of practical skills, these artisans play an essential role in maintaining the integrity of our possessions and enhancing the sentimental value that accompanies them".

Have you ever repaired any famous people's shoes?

"I was working for a big company in Telford Town Centre, and we used to close at nine o'clock in the evenings, and we had to do nights. At about seven o'clock, I was working at the heel bar, and this guy came up to me and said, "Excuse me mate...can you heal me wife's shoes?" and I turned around because the machine was around me, and I said "ok", and I turn around, and I think "I know that voice", but I can't think who it is. I turn around, and I notice that the guy has a purple bit on his beard right here...and then I think, "I know who it is...it's Roy Wood!" I said, "There you go, pal", and he said,

"Thank you very much", and off he went. Another night, Eddy Kidd, the stunt cyclist, was in Telford Town Park and jumping over a few things one weekend. We had two chairs, and he sat down on one of them and said, "Can you heel these?" I said, "Yes"; they were his cowboy boots, and he took them off and gave them to me. At that time, there was a dry cleaner next to where I was, and all the women were saying, "Ooh...look who it is!" Anyway, so I carried on doing his heels and charged him, and he was very serious, so off he went. He must have been preparing mentally for his jump!"

What is the history of your shop?

"Before being a cobbler's, this was a sweet shop and then a cake shop owned by Mrs Jeffreys, a local lady who is still my landlady. She comes and visits me every Thursday. It was a butcher's in the 1940s; before that, it was a courtyard for a pub".

Do you have any other interests?

"My daughter just played buttons in a local production, and I was also in it...I wore make-up for the first time and did some singing and dancing in the chorus".

Chapter Four

Mark's Barbers

There once was a barber, a star,

Whose haircuts were known near and far.

With each snip and trim,

He brought joy to each whim

and his customers all sang, "Hurrah!"

Can you let me know your name and the name of your business?

"This is a traditional gentleman's barber's not that most of the people that come here are gentlemen, but most of them are! I've been here 17 years, I think now... in Bell Street Wellington. And my business does what it says on the tin! The pandemic had a big effect on business because everyone stayed at home and they all just sort of cut their hair the best they could, and it was good enough at the time. However, now they are starting to return and visit again on a regular basis? There are now several barbers operating within Wellington, but I'm the only one that provides a traditional service. I began my journey as an apprentice, mastering straight-razor shaves and precise scissor cuts. Over time, I embraced new trends and advanced techniques, constantly evolving my craft. My clients range from older gentlemen who appreciate a classic cut and shave to younger patrons seeking the latest styles".

What does being a barber mean to you?

"Being a barber to me is more than just cutting hair - it's about creating an entire experience. In my chair, engaging conversations flow naturally, whether it's about local happenings or personal stories. I strive to make every visit to my barbershop a fusion of tradition and modernity, a warm environment that keeps clients coming back. In Wellington, being a traditional barber means upholding the timeless art of the trade while meeting contemporary preferences. I work to strike this harmony, giving each client a journey through the

rich history and exciting future of barbering, making them feel valued and part of our shared heritage".

What do you mean by the term "traditional barber"

"The history of barber shops and the art of barbering is fascinating and dates back to ancient civilizations when barbers were responsible for cutting hair and providing various grooming and therapeutic practices. As time passed, the role of barbers evolved, and by the 19th century, dedicated barber shops became hangout spots for men, offering meticulous grooming and a chance to socialize. The atmosphere was all about camaraderie and tradition. Rituals like hot towel shaves, precise scissor cuts, and attention to detail in styling became staples of the barbershop experience. These places go beyond just grooming; they embody a cultural connection across generations, creating a sense of continuity and shared heritage. Moreover, the ritualistic nature of the barbering experience, from the soothing lather of a shaving cream to the precise snip of the scissors, has a therapeutic effect. The act of self-care and grooming in a traditional barbershop is a moment of respite from the hustle and bustle of everyday life. It allows individuals to pause, reflect, and indulge in a sensory experience beyond the aesthetic outcome. The sensory elements, including the scents of tonics and aftershaves, the tactile sensation of a skilled barber's touch, and the ambient sounds of clippers and conversation, contribute to a holistic well-being that transcends the physical realm".

"Barbershops have a rich history and are a hub for cultural heritage, community, and personal well-being. They celebrate

tradition, craftsmanship, and the importance of human connection in our lives. In today's world, they still play a crucial role in fostering community and well-being. Getting a haircut isn't just about looks; it's also about our mental and emotional well-being. A barber shop's cosy setting and personal attention create a space for heartfelt conversations and real connections. It's a place where men can share stories, talk about life, and build relationships with their barbers and other customers. This sense of togetherness positively impacts mental health, providing a supportive community for individuals to find comfort and connection."

How did you develop your professional hairdressing skills?

"I was taught barbering by Peter Pyne, my wife's uncle. He was a British and European champion and coached the British Hairdressing Team when they won the top award. I was lucky enough to train under him when I first started doing this".

Have you noticed the town improving in recent years?

"The town of Wellington has seen significant improvements, largely thanks to the efforts of "Love Wellington" and the support of the local council. Their work has brought life back to the streets and led to the flourishing of new businesses. The "Makers Dozen" mural, created by Rob Francis, has played a significant role in drawing attention to the town and encapsulates Wellington's spirit of creativity. Moving forward, continued growth while maintaining the town's distinctive character is important. The implementation of more community events, cultural initiatives, and environmentally sustainable practices could further

enhance the town's vibrancy and appeal to residents and visitors. This collective effort aims to ensure that Wellington remains a great place to visit".

Do you have any funny stories about your customers that you are willing to tell?

"I used to have one customer from Wrexham who wanted the insignia of Wrexham shaved into his haircut. Unfortunately, he couldn't keep still in the barber's chair, so trying to meet his particular demands was a great challenge. I also used to have a lovely customer called Mike, who had his hair cut here for years and years. We always got on well and had a laugh. One day, he came in and sat in the waiting chair while I was cutting a gentleman's hair. I said, "Hello, Mike. You look a bit rough today. Are you alright?"

And he said, "I'm fine."

I asked, "Are you sure?"

He replied, "I'm fine; leave me alone."

I insisted, "Mike, you look like you're at death's door, and I know someone who can help you with that!" As I said that, I whipped the gown off the customer in the chair, revealing that it was a vicar having his hair cut! Anyway, the vicar got up, and as Mike took his turn to sit in the chair, the vicar gave him a card and said, "Here you are, Mike... just in case!"

Chapter Five

The Gaming Café

There once was a bright spark called Jon,

whose knowledge of games was bar none;

with energy and finesse,

he played Kerplunk and chess,

and his customers all had some fun!

Can you let me know your name and the name of your business?

"My name is Jon Drew, and our business is the boardroom gaming café here in New Street Wellington. We are a gaming café, and we strive to create a safe space for a community of people who just want to come and be part of something and just sit down and discuss. We do not shy away from computer games; we love computer games and the way that the future's going; you can't stop that stream train…it's going to happen. However, we do love the idea of sitting around a table and using tangible things like game pieces, rolling the dice and taking a chance on the Monopoly board. We currently host about six hundred games, and when we opened on the fifth of March in 2022, we started with eighty-nine games. The truth of the matter is that I have only bought another sixty…and the rest have been donated to us by community members, or we have bought in charity shops. When I say we have bought games, I mean that we have bought old games and made them new, or people have just come in and said, "Would you like these? These have been in my cupboard".

Can you be specific about the types of games you have received?

"We always get the classics like Monopoly, and I must have at least ten copies of Kerplunk, where you have to release the sticks and the marbles fall down…I must have at least ten copies of those. There are so many…we have a vast array. We have one gentleman who still comes in and visits us, and he has become a friend of the café, and he personally donated one hundred and five board games! Some of them valuing from ten pounds to three hundred and fifty pounds. He still comes in and visits me, and he has donated up to one hundred and seventeen games. Bless him!"

So, people can come in and choose which game to play while enjoying coffee, food, and a convivial atmosphere.

"Yes, it's all about board games, and we also have a wide range of electronic game consoles, things that date back to the late nineties and eighties, and we actually hold retro gaming events where people can come and play on the old consoles and enjoy using old cartridges and all that. We don't actually promote computer gaming, although we have the ability to, but we do offer birthday parties and packages where you can play computer games. However, our main focus is the café first and foremost and creating a community…we just happen to have six hundred board games".

Can you tell me something about your background in business?

"I was born in Wolverhampton and moved to Telford when I was nine…. I haven't left since then and have enjoyed my time. I have always worked in Telford other than a small stint in Birmingham, and I have worked in the Ironbridge Gorge Museums and volunteered there for some time, as well as the

Black Country Museum. This was all education-based material, and I was learning programming. I have always worked with children and families and have always been keen on making those memories and fun times, and that's what we are trying to do here essentially".

As I speak to you, I can see that some children at the back have picked some board games from the shelves and are going to play with them, including their parents.

"We love Wellington because when we chose this town, and this is the truth...we had a jokey conversation between my wife, Jennifer and my two brothers, Luke and Jacob and sat down in early 2022, and we said...if we were to open a business together, what would it be? And we all said if I may use air quotations, "a nerd café," and we all thought, "That sounds like fun". Then in a few weeks of that discussion, we had registered a business and opened a bank account, and we were looking at properties, and we were looking everywhere, and we were stood in Wellington one day, and we were looking at where the cycle shop is now, and there was one just a bit higher up in New Street, and we hadn't even seen this place, and the estate agent was saying "We've got this place and it's just around the corner from the market and do you want to have a look?" We walked into thirteen New Street where we are now and I just said "Yes, this is it!" And they showed us the rest of the building and I was like "Yes, this is it!" I didn't realise at first, but the business became more than a business...it became a community, we never realised how much more it was going to become and now we are all about community and that is how our business has grown".

Do you know what this building was before?

"It was Holland and Barrett before us...my wife has been doing some research into the property. She found out that it was a pharmacy at one point, and there was a cobbler upstairs. Originally, it was known as "The Bell's Pub." It turns out that Bell Street was called Bell Street because the charity shop next door and this building used to be one building".

What about the pandemic? How did that affect your business plans?

"I'm not sure if Holland and Barrett closed before the pandemic or during it, but it was empty for a little while before we came along. So, we started after the pandemic, and there were things going on at my wife's place and how it had gone during the pandemic...it wasn't that great, and my brothers were in a bit of a weird spot as well due to that as well. In contrast, I was quite happy cruising along doing what I was doing and all of a sudden, I ended up here!"

What do you think contributed to the reemergence of Wellington?

"The building and the location are great, but to be honest with you, we were very blessed with the "Thrive and Revive" High Street grants to help us find the business, and it paid for the entire counter you can see over there and the bits and bob's. The Council and "Love Wellington" if there was anything that I needed, I have just rung them up, and they have said, "Here..." There was a moment, a business blip, and I was stressing, and I had people come and see me to see if I was okay!"

How do you see Wellington developing in the future, and what would you like to see?

"I think it's on a climb...I think it's on the right path now with the Council taking over the market; I think that that is a big event, and that is going to be absolutely brilliant and getting that pushed even more. They are doing some work on the buildings to get them back to not just being respectful but also being a nice, comfortable place. I think that new businesses need to look at Wellington as not just a place of property but a community where people will shop, and businesses will be part of it. For example, I ran the pancake race this morning, and we had five businesses turn up and be part of events, and they were gracious enough to be part of a community event".

I notice that you have some slogans that are printed on your leaflets

"Yes, we have two, actually. The main one is the business-focused one, which is "Meet, eat, game, repeat!" We also like to say that we want people to come here and be their unapologetic selves. That is why we hang the pride flag in the window all year round, and we welcome neurodivergence as well as all neuro spicy. We also have children with their superpowers, and we just want people to come here and be safe and comfortable".

Do you have any anecdotes about customers or the things that they ask for?

"Well, there is nothing in particular that I can remember, but people do come in, and they want to make us laugh and be part of the community. We went to an event called "Comic Con", where we represented the gaming café, and people came from all over the country. We took about a hundred games with us and giant chess and things...and we know we couldn't handle everything ourselves, so I asked around, and twenty members of our community gave up their free time and put café aprons on and played random games with people. That's what we've got, and that's something that I am very proud of. That was in Telford at the International Centre, and it was a good opportunity to promote Wellington and everything that we do here".

Sheldon Cooper from "The Big Bang Theory" would have been very proud...

"He would have been...in fact, we have that game!" (Laughter)

What about the food you sell? Are there any aspects of it that are unique to your business?

"Well, you know, in many places, customers are afraid to ask for this and that or anything extra or anything being taken off. All of our menu is built...you can have what you want on your toasty. You can ask for what you want...do you want it on white or brown bread, or you want ham without the cheese, or do you want vegetarian or vegan? We have cheesecakes...we have imported noodles that we put in a special bowls...we have bubble teas...we have Chinese, Japanese, and Taiwanese. We just have titbits that people can try and enjoy. The honest truth is that we couldn't do this without any of our staff. Including my sister-in-law, who just happens to be over there! (Laughter). We wouldn't have the pancakes for the event today without Helen, and we wouldn't have the Pokémon community if it wasn't for Emma. I could go on and on, and each staff member brings something to it, and since we have been open for two years, we have only had one staff member leave! They have all stayed here...this is a hospitality business...people do not hang around in the hospitality business, but here they love it".

"In terms of our business paradigm, we realise that we couldn't survive on just this business alone, so we have developed a learning department, and between myself and my sister-in-law, we actually have thirty-two years of experience of teaching outside of the classroom and science-based museums such as the Blist's Hill, Black Country Museum, and the Sealife Centre. We love doing education programmes and working with the Council; we do "Rockets in the Park", where we were launching paper rockets that went, goodness me, about eighty metres or even a hundred metres across the park. We do the "City Centre Science Show" in the Church at Christmas, and I have done what they call "The Victorian

Street Games" in the town square. It's just about making games from stuff you can find around the house. The one I like the best is the one where you get a bucket and a coin between their knees and, waddle along, and then drop it into the bucket...I call that game "Spend a Penny". We created a programme called "R.O.L.L.", which is "Roll on Link Learning" in schools, primary educators and homes...or just in the local area. Amongst all the things we do during the week and repeat and all of our other things...we just like to exhaust ourselves!"

Chapter Six

The Guitar Vault

There once was a man with a vision,

His shop, "The Vault," his grand mission

With guitars on the walls and pedals galore

He created a magical space

With precision

Can you let me know your name and the name of your business?

"My name is Jake Taylor, and I'm the owner of the Guitar Vault in Wellington"

What kind of things do you sell in your shop?

"I buy and sell second-hand guitars and guitar-related equipment, and I also repair and renovate guitars and sell them. I saw all kinds of guitars, but I tend to like the more unusual shapes and weird pickup configurations... so not necessarily Fenders and Gibsons, although if I can find them overseas, they are always popular... but I do like the weird and wonderful. One example of this is the "EKO flying V" that I have in the shop... so with that one I stock EKO guitars, and they have been around since the 1960s; a lot of people don't realise that they are still going, and they have recently started distributing again in the UK and when the rep comes around I always check to see what weird models he's got in storage and occasionally he comes in with some odd one's for me because not a lot of guitar shops want to take them. That one came in a few months ago, and I fell in love with it because it is so strange. I also enjoy other unusual guitars, such as the Russian guitars and the soviet era guitars, because of their mental shapes. So, at the time, they didn't have access to all the parts, and all guitars they saw on television were broadcast from America, so that's all they had to go on when they were designing these things, and some of them are just *totally bizarre, similar in a way to Hagstrom guitars which used accordion materials. I think they just had to use what they had, and some of it was old military equipment. That's why they had weird six-pin connectors instead of normal input jacks, bizarre shapes, and big chunky military switches".*

Are there some makes of guitars that customers seem to like?

"Both these Russian guitars and the Eko guitars are retro-futurist, and some customers really like that. I just remembered that a friend of mine has an old soviet era effects pedal, and it's massive! Like the size of a...tank! All of the controls are in Russian, and you have no idea what you're changing. There are all these chunky knobs and faders, and it sounds great, but it's kind of a lucky dip, really. There's an app on your phone, and you can scan and translate things. We were scanning the controls and trying to translate what to do with it. I also sell guitar pedals that enhance and sometimes radically change the sound...you can never have enough pedals! I have lots of wild pedals...overdrive pedals, filter pedals, and a couple of synthesizer pedals which make your guitar sound like an analogue synthesizer. I have a pitch shifter, one that makes your guitar sound like an organ, wah's, volume pedals, and all sorts of other things. I have a Morely wah somewhere, and the Electro Harmonics pedals are still made in America".

How do you think Wellington is doing at the moment?

"In terms of surviving the doughnut effect, I think Wellington hasn't got many big-name shops, but it does have a lot of independent shops, which I think has helped, and we have Telford Town Centre for all of that, really, so I think that people come to Wellington for that experience. Also, it's easy to get to Wellington. You can get to it by train or bus, and the car park is free, so it's quite easy to get down and visit it. Also, historically, I believe that it used to be the centre of the area before it became Telford New Town. I think that people still think of Wellington and Oakengates as being part of the centre of the area, even though there is a Telford Town Centre now. An important part of the way in which Wellington survived the doughnut effect has to be down to the work of "Love Wellington" and Wellington council, as well as the Orbit cinema. Not many people have their own independent cinema, which I think is great. I think that the Orbit cinema has achieved great things!"

How do you think that the town coped with the pandemic"

"In terms of the pandemic, I think everybody struggled a bit at the time I was in the Wellington market, and because it was locked down, I was unable to get to any of my stock. For me, it was a struggle anyway. However, after lockdown, everybody seemed to put a lot of thought into where they were buying things from, and there seemed to be a big surge towards

independent retailers. After the pandemic, people seemed to enjoy being in the fresh air and having an outdoor shopping experience. People don't appreciate things until they are taken away, and I think there was a paradigm shift in the first year, and then people started to get into their old habits again, but people are still a bit more conscious of where they buy things from. A lot of people are saying that they are trying not to buy from Amazon if possible and avoid buying online, but unfortunately, sometimes there is no other option for these days. I really like niche shops...I really miss Maplin's; it always had the little bits I needed, and I can't always find them so easily now. They had everything I needed in one place to complete repairs and build things. It was an inventor's paradise, no doubt about that. I used to get my parts from there sometimes, but I can see why they went under, as I was only buying three transistors for about 50p!"

How do you feel about the recent revival of the town?

"Creativity played a key role in surviving the doughnut effect, and you can see that in the kinds of independent shops that have sprung up in Telford. The late-night events at Wellington Market have been an enormous success and have been very busy. Absolutely packed with people coming from everywhere to enjoy the entertainment, food, and atmosphere of the old market. It is the market that kept it all going. The late-night market started after I left and moved my business into the town, but I have been a few times, and it has always been ridiculously busy. On one occasion when I went down, my

brother's band was playing, and it was so busy that I couldn't get in - it was great, and they do comedy events as well. The Orbit cinema has also done a great job of bringing the square to life. They had "Chitty Chitty Bang Bang", and they also had one of the James Bond cars and the DeLorean from "Back to the Future".

Do you have any funny stories about customers that you can tell us about?

"On a humorous note, there are a list of banned songs that music shop owners do not want their customers to play. This includes "Smoke on the Water" by Deep Purple and "Wonderwall" by Oasis…it can be soul-crushing to hear these several times a day. I am thinking of getting a security guard to deal with such matters or a punnet of ripe tomatoes. There was an occasion when my mum was looking after the shop, and a man came in and wanted to sell her his tennis racket, which I thought was quite good. I think he thought we bought second-hand items and probably didn't notice that we had rather a large collection of guitars!"

Chapter Seven

Leslie's Larder

Wellington, Shropshire, The Road to Revival

In a market where vendors all play,

A cheese lady brightens our day.

With Brie and with Cheddar,

Shropshire Blue, even better,

Her smile chases grey clouds away!

Can you let me know your name and the name of your business?

"My name is Lisa Longland, and I am the current owner of Leslie's Larder; it just so happens that the real Leslie of Leslie's Larder has come to help me. So, there is the founder of the business over there…my mum! So that is the founder who started the business, but we sort of started the business together, but my children were very young, so I started part-time and over the years, as my children have grown up and become independent and my mum has become older and wanted to retire, and that's the reason that I'm here on my own usually…but she has popped in to help me today. Throughout the lockdown, which is almost four years ago now to the day, in the very beginning of the pandemic, the market was forced to close by its owners at the time, but through popular demand, we were asked if we would re-open…certainly the food sections that were open at the time because the supermarkets were open and why couldn't we?

So, I came back to work after only eight weeks off, and it was quite surreal. There was hardly anyone in here, so when anyone approached the market stall, I probably hadn't talked to anyone for half an hour or so, so I pounced on them and became their friend".

Hence the reason for your loyal customers…

"Probably!"

"Well, I think…do you remember the term "we were allowed exercise" and so through that little hour in the day, people would come out and find me, and they decided that they wanted to shop

in the market and even when they had the opportunity to shop in the supermarket, they decided that they would like to support smaller independent people rather than the conglomerates. So, I think that my business is much much stronger since that period of time and I have to say that we kept the market going and it was only me, the "cheese lady" with jams, pies, and cheese etc... And there was, of course, the butcher, the baker, there wasn't a candlestick maker unfortunately".

"Wellington council, I love Wellington...everyone upped their game, and the whole shop local thing started to happen. And, of course, the council applied more recently for that start-up grant, which they won and with most of the money they were given, they purchased the market. Hopefully, that's a positive, and they will be able to put money into the market to bring the building up to standard. They've got the stall holders and a good mix of people. I don't think there are any empty stalls in the market at the moment, which is fantastic and also, we have been doing the late nights, which have been very successful".

Can you tell me about some of your products like the one I used to buy?

"Do you mean the "Shropshire Blue"? Yes, of course. When we started the business, there were two things that were important to us, The first one was the quality of the product, and the second was that we wanted the product to be as local as we could. And you have immediately picked the "Shropshire Blue", which everyone assumes is from Shropshire but actually isn't...it's from Gloucestershire! It is now man-made in Gloucestershire, but it was developed in Scotland! I am almost certain that it was first called "Argyle Blue", but it wasn't very popular, so he renamed it Shropshire Blue in honour of our beautiful county!"

After the "Blue remembered hills" in the poem "A Shropshire Lad" by A.E. Housman?

"That's it! Anyway, so that's where it comes from "Shropshire Blue" and the "Shropshire lad". So, everyone comes here and says, " Ooh…I don't live here, but I must take away something that's local, and they always ask for "Shropshire Blue", and of course, it isn't, but we do have a local cheese producer in the county called Mr Mointon, and all of his cheeses are available here. Ten or more customers come here every week, and they ask me for my favourite cheese, and it's "Worcester Gold", and I think I should be on commission because I sell loads of it, and when people come to the counter, and they are new, I always offer a taste of cheese because it's not cheap these days and it's no use buying a great lump if you haven't tasted it first. Therefore, I am always happy to offer a taste of the cheeses, and I say, "Well, start with this one…this is my favourite", and that rarely fails, and most people go home with a piece, and I always suggest that if they come back and cannot remember the name of the cheese, they can ask me about my favourite cheese!"

Can you tell me something about the craft of cheese-making?

"Making cheese is like a centuries-old art form, and it's all about turning milk into something amazing. It's a mix of science and creativity, where the cheesemaker carefully *guides milk through a bunch of steps to create a flavourful and long-lasting product. This involves balancing bacteria and enzymes, controlling temperature and humidity, and relying on the cheesemaker's gut instincts. And get this - it's not just about the end result! Cheese-making respects local landscapes and cultures, resulting in lots of different types of cheese. Plus, there's a focus on using local ingredients and practices that support the environment. So, making cheese isn't just about the delicious outcome; it's a whole journey that connects us to our roots. That's one of the reasons I love selling cheese because it connects with my customers a proud tradition".*

Do customers ever ask you for unusual things?

"One of the most popular things that are on sale has always been the Samosas, now I have many, many customers who go back years, and one of them is an elderly gentleman who came along and began asking me for a satsuma and I said, "Oh my darling…I don't sell them, but there's a vegetable stall across the road I'm sure they sell them". He continued, "No, you do sell them!" I said that I would take him across the road, but he was insistent: "You do sell them…chicken ones!". Then the penny dropped, and I realised that he meant a chicken samosa and not a chicken satsuma"

How would you describe your ideal customer?

"My ideal customer is someone who comes along, purchases good-quality food, and has a nice chat with me while they are here".

Chapter Eight

Gratitude Café

In the heart of the town, a delight,

A cafe where joy feels just right.

With gratitude near,

For mornings so clear,

Where coffee and calmness unite.

Could you let me know your names and the name of your business

"We are Michelle Busby and David Busby, and we are the owners of the Gratitude Café".

Why is it called the Gratitude Café, and what are you so grateful for?

David: "One of the artists who got me into music and enjoyed it when I got into playing the guitar was Jason Mraz, who wrote a song about "Gratitude Café" which is in California. Michelle always wanted to open a café, and the cafe in California is a music café".

Michelle: "We wanted to bring that sort of Californian vibe to Wellington, and we're almost there! Jason Mraz is a worldwide superstar. Every time that song comes on, and we hear the line about taking a table at the Gratitude Café, we think that's it; that's why we're here!"

It looks great, and I'm very impressed with how you created a café and performance space. How did you achieve this?

Michelle: "I was literally on maternity leave with our second child. I was at home baking and going to coffee shops with friends, and I just thought, "I wonder if I could do this?" Do the baking and the coffee shop vibe and never had the guts to go for it. I was working a nice, steady job in the NHS, and it was secure with a good future. There were also lots of changes planned and constant rounds of redundancies and restructuring, and I just thought, "I will be in charge of all this anyway. It was David who gave me the confidence and the push because I don't think I would have ever gone into it had they not forced me out or made me redundant, which they were never going to do".

Because of that, I can sit here in Wellington and have a cappuccino while listening to Carlos Santana. What more could anyone want?

Michelle: *"Well, yes, exactly and in Wellington!"*

Are you both from Shropshire originally?

Michelle: *"Yes, we are both from Shropshire".*

David: *"I'm a Dawley man".*

When did you start to put your plan into action?

Michelle: *"My son is now 15, and I didn't have the guts until 8 years ago. I handed in my notice, and then it was the case of finding the right premises. It was a big do-up job, and we did it all ourselves without any redundancy money. This place has been open for nearly 6 years, and we were one of the first new businesses to open. It was really strange because everyone who came in said, "This is exactly what Wellington needs" and it made me feel really proud because we knew that is what Wellington needed".*

Michelle: *"There were some cafes with a sort of greasy spoon image, but that's not what we wanted to do".*

David: "*Some people said, "Not another café." But we wanted something with more of an artistic vibe that was also a venue...somewhere that represents an artistic and creative space for people".*

Michelle: "*That was going to be our strapline "We are more than just a café." We are both creative people and musical and that's why we do workshops and events".*

The problem with being a forward thinker is that you have to wait for the world to catch up. Have you found this to be the case?

"Yes, these first two years were a real slog, and then there was Covid..."

Well, before we move on to that, looking around, I have to congratulate you on a real success story; you and some other businesses I have interviewed represent a new era for the town in a way that compliments established businesses.

Michelle and David: "Thank you".

You had just started, and then the pandemic came along; how was that for you?

Michelle: "It was horrific. We had to have a really frank conversation with our accountant about whether we could actually survive. And to be quite frank, if it wasn't for the government grant, we wouldn't have made it. Then there was the Government's Bounce Back Scheme, and without it, we would have really struggled. It was the same for everyone; we saw so many businesses struggle not just in Wellington but in Telford, and I thought, I don't want to be one of those. So, we just threw everything into it, and as soon as restrictions were lifted, we just thought, "How can we improve the menu? How can David do more music events? How can we get the youth back in? Just so many ideas".

What did you have to do during the pandemic to keep things going?

Michelle: *"We did take-away only, and I was here on my own, which was the most depressing thing ever!"*

You put some blues music on...

Michelle and David: (Laughter)

Michelle: *"It was the strangest of times, and David took our music events online, which was absolutely amazing".*

David: *"It was just me playing to a camera, and the way I played music changed completely. I couldn't play with a band, so I started using a looper pedal, and it has actually made a big difference to how I perform. So, if it wasn't for Covid, I wouldn't be doing what I'm doing now".*

Who is your favourite guitarist?

"It wouldn't be a favourite guitarist, I'm more into singer/songwriters, but I'm inspired by people like Jack Johnson and Jason Mraz. I do play a lot of Ed Sheeran at the moment

because he's so popular and can use the looper pedal like he does. Getting back to that song about the Gratitude Café, it's about a chilled vibe and music like Jack Johnson and Jason Mraz, which, even if you don't know their music, you can enjoy and say, "I really like the message in this." It's more about the artist than a specific guitarist, although Jason Mraz is actually a really good guitar player".

What kind of music events do you run here?

David: "We do music on Sundays, and we are bringing back the open mic night on Thursdays. I cut my teeth on open-mic nights, playing three songs and being nervous as hell while doing it. Open mic events are great for playing in front of people and finding contacts and stuff. In terms of events here, because I play weddings and festivals over the summer, it's usually only Sundays that I put events on, so you have to follow our Facebook or Instagram to see what's going on".

The business owners I have interviewed often love stories. There's a book or a concept album for you, actually...

David: (Laughter) "I should write some songs about it!"

There is also a nice family atmosphere here. Is that connected to what you do in the café?

David: "Whenever I build anything at home, or projects for other people, or when I build or decorate a venue, or build a place that people are going to sit or just constantly look around or the angles in a wall…something interesting to sit in. Just somewhere where people can sit together; I just like to see people come together".

This place is beautifully decorated, and there are so many interesting things to look at while we are sitting here. Who did all this?

"All me…Michelle picked out all the wallpapers and things, but every screw in the wall is me".

How long did it take?

"About three months!"

Where did you get your design ideas?

David: "From the shape of the building, I'm not much of a planner, but I do work well in the moment. This building has been lots of things. Before we took it over, it was a music shop. In fact, I used to teach music with the person who was in here, and I said to him "We should open a little café in the corner" in this exact building, and he said, "No, I don't want to do that" and when he left the idea was kind of abandoned, and you had bands coming in and out. So, when it came through, and we owned this place, I said "Yeah, we'll have a café." Because it was a music shop, I think that music's in the building".

You are to be congratulated, and you even have a great view out of the window of a classic Wattle and Daub wall to look at while enjoying a meal or a coffee.

David: "It wasn't always that way; when that building was empty, there was graffiti on the wall, but it's been removed now and returned to its original condition".

That's good…we want a Californian vibe and not New York!

"Yes, it was an urban New York Vibe when we moved in, but we've changed that!"

When did you notice a change in Wellington? Was it noticeable when you moved in?

David: "My first thought was, "Are we going to do this in Wellington?" It's a historic market town, but no matter how nice a town, how nice the buildings are it's the people that make it. It's the people in Wellington that have been so supportive and the thing I have noticed is that the people in Wellington love Wellington. And I think that Wellington is rising up with the Market being taken over by the council and the new independent shops opening. You get a lot more outside people coming to the town these days".

How would you like to see Wellington developing in the future?

David: "When events are put on in The Square, they really do help to bring people into the town; I would just like to see more. I don't want to say young or modern events, but The Square could be used a bit more, and it could have a stage. If you look at a place like Shrewsbury using things to attract visitors...it's usually music and food. The shops are there, obviously keeping people shopping, but it's usually the cultural events that attract people to a town. Initially, when they started doing the late-night market, I was brought in to organize the stage and the music, and now it's one of the major events in Wellington. People flocked there because there was food there and there were bands on. There was food, drink, and music. and you've only got to see the success of the late-night market to see that that has to be brought into the whole town. So, there could be more of that brought into The Square. I arranged the music for the first late-night market event, and we didn't know if it was going to work, and it just went massive! We just need to bring that into the square and create the same kind of atmosphere which will then benefit the town in a wider context. I would be happy to get involved with making that happen if the council was interested!"

Are there any other things you would like to see happening in Wellington in the future?

Michelle: *"Mirroring what David said, there are other market towns that are thriving, like Shrewsbury, like Bridgenorth, and as he said it is really about those events. They aren't isolated to one particular part of the market. They are in the square, in the high street and in the side streets. That's the way it should be, not just bits and bobs, but the whole of Wellington. The other important thing that would help bring people in would be the parking; it's only two hours in the car park by Wilkos, and it used to be three. If you look at what's going on in the outskirts of Wellington, we're going to get a lot of families coming in, aren't we and could do with something that catered to families...such as, I don't know, one of those bowling alley-type things and some outdoorsy stuff, obviously not too far away but something in the centre of town. Perhaps there could be more outdoor performing arts events where families could enjoy their time together in Wellington".*

Chapter Nine

Spinning Records

Wellington, Shropshire, The Road to Revival

There once was a woman of note,

Who opened a store to promote,

Her love of rare vinyl,

And record revival,

And "Swifties" soon found their top spot!

Can you let me know your name and the name of your business?

"My name is Emma Perks, and I am the owner of spinning around records".

When did you open your business?

"I opened in September, so I am still fairly new to the high street, but it also feels like a lifetime! I have always had an interest in collecting vinyl, and this time around, I have been collecting vinyl since 2015. I've got a thing where I absolutely love pop music and being a woman…so it's two things that don't normally go together with record shops, to be honest. When my job where I was before got sent abroad, I decided to take the advanced payoff they were offering and open a record shop that taps into all of those things that most record shops don't! In specific terms, pop music is at the forefront of what I do in contrast to other types of record shops that are into what I would call "man rock", and there's nothing wrong with "man rock", but I just like to celebrate pop music. That's not to say that you can't find the traditional types of rock music amongst the racks in the shop; it's just that pop music is really at the centre of what I do here. My ideal customers are the younger ones who are just getting into collecting now, and they can find it intimidating to go into a lot of your regular record shops; they can come in here, and I am friendly, and I know a lot about my pop music, and they find it comfortable to come in. I cater for a wide range of pop collectors, because again, I

get the latest releases which are sometimes ignored by other record shops...but really my customers can be anybody! I think I started out with an idea about what I wanted to do, and I have so many customers within the footfall that I'm always happy to order anything that someone might be looking for. I think it's an ethos of what I do that you don't judge or laugh at anyone in regard to their musical taste".

How is it going since you began trading?

"All interest is welcome, and it seems to be going down really well. everyone is really pleased to see a record shop back on the High Street. I have a life-size image of Taylor Swift in the window... she's my number one! It's great to see young music fans enjoying her work and filling stadiums around the world. Her fans are always welcome in this shop I do know that one of my favourites, of course, is Kylie. Kylie Minogue's music has inspired the name for this shop that's why it's called "Spinning Around Records". Her album was the first album I ever owned and that's a special moment in any young person's life, the first time you buy music by someone who you really love. I have literally grown up with her in the same way that many music fans today will grow up with Taylor Swift or Billie Eilish. The music of your favourite artist speaks to you in some way and inspires you and supports you; it can be a very rewarding experience... that's what's so great about collecting records. Many young customers are following the trend of buying records because they enjoy the physical nature of owning something that they can hold and share with their friends. It used to be the case that young music fans would sit around discussing album lyrics uncovered with their friends in small groups, and it's great to see that this generation is able to enjoy a similar experience".

Do you have particular artists that you enjoy listening to?

"I love all the ladies of pop, so I've got Taylor Swift, Katy Perry, Lana Del Rey, and they are all scattered around the shop for customers to discover. There has definitely been an emergence of interest in buying vinyl and it has been growing and growing. When I started collecting again this time around, it was just a small box of vinyl from the leading High Street retailer that we won't mention, and it's got to the stage now where you can have a whole shop full of just vinyl. I think it started during the pandemic when people began to get their records out of the attic getting record players and rediscovering how much they loved them. I also think that the younger ones enjoy what we did when you get a big physical product, and you get all the pictures, lyrics, and different coloured vinyl. It's physical, and it's collectable, and you're interacting with it in a way that you don't when you're streaming it. I'm in no way ever a BBC Radio 6 music hipster, and like I say, it's pop music all the way for me. However, I am quite broad in what I know and like in music".

How do you think Wellington doing these days?

"The fact that Wellington has survived what you call the "doughnut effect" is down to several factors. During the pandemic, we all got quite lazy and ordered things online because, in many cases, we had no choice. Therefore, for a while, we just got into the habit of it and thought to ourselves, "Well, I don't have to go out of my house… I'll just order it on the Internet". But then you could see so many businesses going out of business just because of that, and now people realise that if you don't shop local and support traders, even if it's on the Internet because I sell a lot online… they like buying from me because they know I'm a small business. I think customers understand that if you don't support local businesses, you're going to lose them. So, I think that that has had a big effect now, and I've noticed that they don't want to order online, and they want to come in, and they want to buy from a physical shop because they realise what a difference that makes. People have realised that they don't want to be a ghost town like Wellington was a few years ago; they want to have a thriving town again with lots of shops to go to, and they can get everything on their doorstep. For me, I grew up in Wellington, so I remember in the heyday when you had all your Woolworths, and John Menzies. I remember hanging out in John Menzies because I wasn't cool enough to hang out at Langdon's record shop. Those were the two places for me on both Woolworths and John Menzies selling the pop records that I loved. Whereas my brother, who was into heavy metal, was at Langdon's and remembers all those days and going into "Partners" and looking at the stationary; it's all about getting back to those days when you can come down, and there are all these businesses".

Do you work with any other businesses?

"I think as a community in the High Street, we all do band together, and we all want to make Wellington work, and it's got free parking as well! You can't go wrong with free parking! I think that "Love Wellington" under the council have made a significant contribution. In fact, without the council, I wouldn't have been able to open my business because although I have some of my own funds to put into this venture, I did get a startup grant for it, which was extremely helpful. So, they have really invested in getting shops back onto the High Street. I know there are still people who haven't visited us in a long, long time and think that Wellington is just nail bars and charity shops Do you want to come and have a look around and see how many different businesses we have got here? There are so many interesting shops to explore, you have a music shop, a book shop, a record shop, an independent cinema, and so many nice eateries. It's just really nice to have a walk around and see what's going on and it's something that's different from the usual. I also think that because many of us are running our businesses ourselves as independent traders, you will get a different type of service than you will from the larger stores. You go into some of the larger stores, and they do not seem that interested, but with smaller stores, you get that personal service from people who love what they do...sole trading with soul. I do remember recording a TikTok in the shop, and a customer walked in asking for a fancy dress costume because they saw the cutouts of pop stars in the window and thought we sold costumes...all as I was filming my TikTok".

How did record store day go last week?

"It was absolutely mental, but it was an amazing success. I didn't know what I was coming into on Saturday morning, but the queue was literally right down the street. And the feedback I got from it has all been amazing and all about how well it was run. Obviously, the nature of the beast was "Record Store Day", and certain lines do sell out, and you don't always have enough for the queue, but on the whole, most people got the bulk of what they wanted. I think it's going to be an even bigger event next year. I know how to run it, and I know that I hold much more stock than other stores locally, so I think I'll be getting a lot more people next year".

You mentioned before how you identified a particular niche in the market

"My niche is always that I am a female-fronted record store that loves pop music. That's what makes me stand out from everywhere else. I've always found that during record store day, people only get 1-2 or three units in, whereas because it's what I deal with, I had masses and masses of them. People were coming from far and wide to come to my store they knew

I was going to have the stock. I had somebody come up from Biddeford in Exeter; she'd been buying online from me but wanted to come up for record store day because she knew I was going to have all the stuff she wanted. We had some other people come down from Wigan because they had what they wanted and they like what I do – they were there from 3:00 in the morning queuing outside my store. That's right; they were queuing at 3:00 in the morning because they knew I only had a few items of that particular stock. The first person was queuing at 12:00 at night. I say I'm a pop record store come up, but he was queuing up for Pearl Jam, so it just goes to show that I sell a wide range of records".

Do you think that people still love to purchase music in this way rather than downloading it?

"Absolutely, to me, it's that you love music, and you love it in a physical format. It doesn't matter what music you like. You don't get judged here because it's all about the fact that you love music and you want it on vinyl. Now that I've got my regulars that I've got to know we discuss music and our favourite albums, the cover artwork and how beautiful the picture disc is…it's enjoying the experience of coming into a record store!"

Now that you've had time to reflect on this year's success is there anything that you'd like to do next year to build on that?

"I think that next year I could still date will be even bigger for me than it has been this year, and the town was really pleased that I brought so many people in – the cafes with people going in for breakfast. People like the little pantry how to busier day because people are coming in with their carrier bags. So, it's just about seeing what I can do next year now that I've run it once; just see if I can make it more of a community event and see what the town can do when so many extra people are going to be coming in".

Chapter Ten

The Little Pantry

Can you let me know your name and the name of your company

"My name is Kelli King, and I am the owner of the Little Green Pantry in Crown Street, Wellington".

Can you let me know the nature of your business and what products and services you offer

"The Little Green Pantry is a zero-waste and re-fill shop, and we are aiming to reduce the plastic waste in people's weekly shopping by offering most of our products as refills. They can bring their own containers and refill as much as they want, and they take home in their own containers, so you are reducing the amount of plastic waste you get from your usual supermarket shop. The range of things we sell...most of our stuff is dried foods, and we have lots of ingredients to make meals, and there are also snacks and lots of dried foods which sell really well".

"We have things like beans and pulses, and we have a range of cleaning liquids that are all eco-friendly, so people can bring their washing-up liquid bottles, for example, and refill them instead of buying a new bottle each time. We have a baking section with things like baking flours, sugars, and chocolates as well as other ingredients. We also have herbs and spices, oils, and vinegars, and a toiletry section and a store cupboard section. There are tinned goods and drinks and things like that, as again, all the toiletries are eco-friendly and in recyclable

packaging. So, there are things like natural toothpaste, deodorants, and soaps".

What gave you the idea for refilling, as that is quite a new idea…

"I started in 2019 after I saw a BBC documentary on "The War on Plastic" where they did a whole street audit on the waste and plastic. They set up recycling bins and put it all out onto the street and counted it all, and it just shocked me how much was accumulating in just one household and on just one street. So, I did that myself at home, and the documentary then follows the recycling process. I actually thought that I was doing quite well by filling my recycling bin every week…but the documentary showed that only a small percentage of that is actually recycled. So, that opened my eyes to becoming more sustainable and reducing my household waste".

How does it work, and what do customers need to do?

"Well, it's a new way of shopping in a way that is eco-friendly and saves you money. It's a refill business model, and how it works is like this…instead of always buying new containers, this model encourages you to reuse your containers and refill your products. It's catching on with companies that sell everyday stuff like cleaning supplies, personal care items, and food. You can bring your own containers to refill stations or buy reusable containers and refill them at a lower cost. This not only cuts down on waste and saves resources, but it also makes you a loyal customer and saves you money in the long run. Plus, it's all about supporting independent shops and the economy and the push for more eco-friendly practices.

Where does this original business model come from?

In 2014, Sara Wolf and Milena Glimbovski teamed up to create Original Unverpackt, the very first zero-waste refill shop in Berlin. With a passion for tackling the problem of single-use packaging, the store offers a wide range of products, from groceries to personal care items, all available in bulk. Customers were encouraged to bring their own containers or use the store's reusable options, helping to cut down on packaging waste. Original Unverpackt became really popular and inspired similar stores all over Europe and even further afield. Thanks to Wolf and Glimbovski's pioneering work, the store not only offers a practical solution for sustainable living but also kick-started a bigger movement towards zero-waste lifestyles. It's still going strong to this day!

How did you start?

"The main idea that sprung out of that was the idea of re-fill shopping. At the time, the nearest one was in Shrewsbury, and I started going over that way and doing my shopping, but I just thought, "I live in Telford, and it's a half-hour drive there, and the car emissions when driving there, and parking meant that it was not that sustainable. It was also a time in my life when I was on maternity leave, and I was looking for something to fit around family life, so I thought that I could start something in Telford. I initially set up a pop-up store to

fit in with my family life, and I popped up at Wellington Market, Newport Market, and local events. Then in 2021, Wellington Council were offering grants to open shops, and I jumped at the chance and thought that this is going to be my one chance to do what I believe is right and hopefully people will want to follow me and live sustainably".

How did you then develop your business?

"As I have said, I started out as a pop-up shop and was moving around Telford, and that gave me the opportunity to do some market research and to see where the busiest and which communities were the most welcoming and open-minded to the idea and Wellington was by far the best when I look back at the figures. It was always the busiest, and we also got a lot of support from "Love Wellington", which is a community group which is all about boosting the positive image of Wellington. So, with the support of "Love Wellington", the Council, and my research, I concluded that it should be the main hub of what I want to do. I would eventually like to move into other towns because we get people in from further afield that do shop here, but it would be nice for them to have something more local as well".

So, is this shop and the way you run it a blueprint for future expansion?

"Yes, that's right".

How was your business affected by the Pandemic?

"Well, I started just before COVID-19, and then there was the lockdown, and all the stalls closed down and all the events I was going to were cancelled. So, I continued to serve my regular customers via a delivery service and me and the kids and I used to pile the car up with things that people had ordered and served them at the door, and people really appreciated that they could still get stuff. So, we carried on in that way until it was safe to return to normal".

Did your children find the delivery service to be a challenge?

"No, they loved it... It was also an excuse to go out while we waited for the lockdown to end".

Chapter Eleven

Wrekin Framers

In the heart of the town, quite a name,

A framer who masters each frame.

With care that's sincere,

For memories dear,

Ensuring they always remain.

Can you let me know your name and the name of your business?

"My name's Phillip Childs and I am part owner with my mate Dave of Wrekin Framers, which some people mix up with "Wrekin Farmers!" There used to be a firm here called "Wrekin Farmers", and people still walk past here and ask, "Are you the farmers?" We make bespoke picture frames. You can easily get frames in other shops in standard sizes, but sometimes they are a bit plasticky, and people want something a bit special. We try to do something at a reasonable price for people; we are not in the habit of ripping people off. It's basically the case that we have a decent turnover of frames and aim to always provide a great service. I also make frames from driftwood and pallets and things like that...natural or recyclable materials. I don't really push that, but people see them on the wall and say, "Can you make us one of those" and we try to put that together. We also stretch canvases, which can be an art in itself, as anyone who has tried to do that will know".

Why do people like framing their pictures and how does it improve their pictures?

"I think it preserves it for one thing, and you couldn't hang it on a way unless it was on in a frame or a stretcher, and it ties in with the décor of a house. Sometimes pictures have a coloured mount around a frame, and they can nicely match the carpet or the curtains or something like that. In fact, interior designers often create a colour scheme for a room

based on colours in a picture above the fireplace or another central position. We want our customers to enjoy their purchase experience, and we provide advice and have a good sense of humour. There is a sign in there that says, "Husbands must bring their wives to choose a frame." You know, because it's a regular occurrence that the gentleman will come in and pick a frame, and the lady comes along and says, "No, no, no…that's not the right one!"

I Notice that you have some humorous frames is there a market for these?

"Yes, there is. There are a few signs that I make at times, and they just catch people's eyes and can help to attract customers. Some customers like to have personalised signs for their gardens or special occasions like anniversaries. Others like to have quotes from famous film stars such as Patrick Swayze. One example would be that one over there. I used to put up a blackboard and write a few humorous comments on it to attract customers, but I haven't done that lately."

It took me a few minutes to get that one. The best jokes are the ones where you think about what you have read and get it a few minutes later.

"Yes…the moonshine one is funny. You would be surprised how many people walk past and are befuddled and how many just burst out laughing!"

Do you and your business partner have a creative background? Why did you choose to go into picture framing?

"No…in another life, I was an electrician, and I didn't want to do the same thing all my life really, and admittedly, I got made redundant at the time that Maggie Thatcher came around, and I had just finished my apprenticeship. I then had to find work and did anything for a while and ended up at Donnington Depot working on military vehicles. Then, in my mid-forties, I had the opportunity to leave, and I did a little bit of travelling for a while, and then after a few years, you need a bit of structure in your life, and I didn't want to do that forever. So, I actually went picture framing in Shrewsbury for a while, and I met Dave, who was in Wellington market, and we used to use the same supplier. After a while, we decided to join forces and do it all in Wellington…so we have been here for about six years or so. The market itself has moved on, so we are glad that we made that decision."

What business was here before?

"It was a furniture business; it used to see Mexican style furniture…Mexican self-assembly that was quite nice, actually, but I believe they went to Halesfield."

How do you think Wellington has survived the doughnut effect when businesses are developed around a town and the centre becomes empty like a doughnut?

"It hadn't survived it like a lot of small towns around here, and Telford and Wrekin Council were keen to promote Telford Town Centre, and all roads lead to the Town Centre quite easily. However, when you go to the smaller towns such as Madely, Oakengates, Dawley, and Wellington, which was always the principal town to go to. I think they have realised that there is a lot more to Telford than Telford Town centre in the last few years, and there has been more investment in some of the other towns, so we can't moan, and things move on, and sometimes they get better."

There has definitely been an improvement in the last few years, and the small businesses have contributed to that. Would you agree?

"I think that's the beauty of the small towns; you don't want too many big stores, really. There might be some people who might want to see a Marks and Spencer's here, but for most people, it's about coming into the market and enjoying the smaller, more personalised shops. You said you had spoken to the guy in the music shop…that's a good example. There are quite a lot of independent shops if people take the time to come and have a look. Coming to Wellington, it can be a morning or afternoon out; you can get a nice cup of coffee around the corner, and there are lots of food places to explore."

Do you have any funny stories about customers you can share?

"**We** do get some customers asking us if we sell bits of wood, which is quite understandable, but there are always funny requests. There is a chap up there that sells all sorts of things and DVDs, and someone this morning asked him if he had a ship's anchor?" There are so many boats around Shropshire, aren't there!?

That's perfect! There aren't enough ship anchors these days…that's a niche market, and I suppose once you buy one, it's going to last you!

Chapter Twelve
The Orbit Cinema

Can you please let me know your name and the name of your business?

"My name is Damian Breeze, and I am the manager of the Orbit Cinema; I am Ray Hughes, and I am the finance, Director".

Can you describe all the things that the Orbit Cinema does?

Damian: *"At the moment, we are a wonderful sixty-three-seater community cinema, and we put on films from the present day, as well as some of the old classics. We are showing "Monty Python and the Holy Grail" at the moment, and we are also a café for the local community selling beautifully hot wonderful food, and we are here for the community".*

Ray…do you have anything else to add?

Ray: *"Well, we have been told that we have the best toilets in Wellington". (laughter)*

Would you call that your Unique Selling Point? Your U.S. Pee!

Damian: *"Not bad…not bad…" (laughter)*

There is an interesting story behind your success, which includes how you tried to save the old Clifton Cinema. Can you tell me something about that?

Ray: *"Basically, what happened was that a group was formed in 2012, which then became a Community Benefit Society in 2013 with the stated aim of providing arts and facilities for the* town, with a particular focus on the Clifton Cinema but that could never be secured, and in 2016 we had an AGM, and members gave us permission to look at alternative venues, and as it happened the HSBC Building cropped up, and it was an affordable price for us, and it was on a lease which was good, so we acquired a lease in 2018 and spent basically a year in constructing what we've got now. So, this is where we are now at the current stage, and what we've got now is plans afoot to develop the upper two floors as well".

Damian: "In fact, we now own the building".

Ray: "Yes, we now own the building without a mortgage-free from debt, and that puts us in a strong position for negotiating for grants and that sort of stuff".

Do you have any more thoughts about the Clifton?

Damian:" Well, I'm not originally from Wellington, I'm from Shrewsbury, and when people come to the Orbit, they think they love this cinema...they think it's fantastic. They do reminisce about the Clifton and how fantastic it was as a cinema in its day and the people queuing around the block to see certain blockbusters and stuff live that. But I think that it's one of those things...it was a great building in its time, and we are moving on from it".

There is a couple on YouTube who explored the Clifton after it was sold. It was empty; there was nothing left inside.

Ray: "*It would have cost an arm and a leg to fix it…we were quoted seven million pounds! And to be honest about that, no granter would give that amount of money to an organisation with no proven track record. Whereas this, as you can see, has proved to be viable and not flourishing*".

You have played a significant part in the revival of Wellington. How about "Love Wellington?" What role do you think they have played?

Ray: "*They came in a bit later, and what you had was a group of directors, of which only two are still on the board for various reasons, including death, unfortunately. They were the people who had the perseverance to get this through. Now we have a board of ten people who are working to the next stage, really*".

And what about the Council's part in this story can you tell me something about that?

"*Wellington Town Council have been particularly supportive of our aims and aspirations from day one. I think that Telford and Wrekin were not enthused by the Clifton project but were enthused by this. In 2018, Telford had its fiftieth anniversary and each of the six towns were granted one hundred and fifty pounds for community projects and that money was all* allocated to us, and since then they have been instrumental in the Capital Regeneration Project Bid, which has effectively given us one point four million pounds to redevelop the upper floors".

What do you think of some of the new businesses that have opened up recently in the town?

Damian: *"Well, going back…we have worked well with both "Love Wellington" and the town council. The council works with us, and we work with them, and "Love Wellington" has done a lot to promote businesses in the town. Regarding new businesses, we have seen them come and go…I mean, we have been here five years this May and while I have been here, I have seen businesses come up and disappear. It's trial and error, but we do seem to be getting some good local independent people who want to bring businesses into town".*

What do you think that any business would need to do to transcend initial start-up and continue successfully?

Damian: *"I'm not sure…it depends on the niche, as you say. We had a Wilko's which is sadly gone, which was a good store where you could get lots of things at reasonable prices. It's now gone into the market in places such as Aladin's Cave that sells all the bits and pieces. So, I think having a variety…I mean, we have a lot of food establishments which is great, but the problem is that you need other things to keep people here. I think one of the downfall's we have at the moment is a lack of* clothes shops, and obviously, with Amazon and online shopping for clothes, it is one of the problems that we are facing".

What about the Pandemic, how did you cope with that?

Damian: *"Well, we survived!"*

"When the pandemic arrived, it was upsetting for everybody and working in any business under those conditions and in particular with this kind of business you do struggle to know what to do. We were shut…we were told to, and we couldn't do anything, so it was hard, it really was".

Ray: *"We had just been here for about nine months and had just got our foothold in the premises, and this hit us, and what saved us was the Culture Recovery Fund which allowed us to make up our shortfall. I was also quite proud of the fact that there were all sorts of furloughs and that we were able to pay all of our staff their full wages. The furlough was eighty per cent all the way through, and also, when we could only open up for a limited period which was for take-away's only, I think it was Fridays and Saturdays…so we were keeping the community going".*

Damian: *"We are not a takeaway, although we can be, so we had to adapt ourselves very well, I thought, and people did come along and use it."*

Ray: *"Yes, and then they relaxed it so you could have outdoor seating, and you could see that there was an appetite for* people to get out of the house, really. So, it worked well for us at that moment in time and people were coming in and sitting outside to eat. Then we were able to open up as a cinema, but with social distancing, we were down from sixty-three to forty at a push. If you got a family together, they could sit together but if it was for one person alone, you could only get about twenty. So, we just built up from there, and I think it has put us back in our development for about two years. But I think we are getting back to where we should be in the next few years, and I think we will get there because of organic growth and an increase in the borough itself which is one of the fastest-growing boroughs for population growth in the United Kingdom. I think that Cambridge was predicted to be bigger than us a one time, and the age of the population is predicted to increase because this is a nice area to retire to, and they would be our core audience and in particular for our afternoon showings. So, we are getting there!"

Damian: "*Just getting back to Covid for a moment, as you know, a lot of businesses closed down, and those were businesses similar to us...cafés and cinemas. A lot of them have not succeeded after Covid which is a sad fact, and for us to be new and still here is fantastic!*"

How do you feel about the success of the late market...were you surprised?

Damian: *"I think it's great...the nightlife in Wellington is not the best as they say. There are pubs and a few late-night restaurants, but not too many proper restaurants. Obviously, we have the new Orange House which opened recently selling Tapas. I don't think that the late-night market does anything for us, but it does bring people into the town who might say, "Oh, there's a cinema there," and they stay open until nine o'clock let's see what they do. Whether it's the late-night market or the things we organise in the square outside our cinema, it gets people in that's the main thing. When we have done events, we have had thousands of people come into town...not necessarily into the Orbit but they go around the town, see something, and come back later on or a week later".*

You put on events in the square can you give me a few examples of what you have organised in the past?

Damian: *"Yes, they were...we do seem to go down the car theme, and I'm running out of ideas! We bought Chitty Chitty Bang Bang to Wellington and showed the film, we've had an Aston Martin here, as well as a similar car to the one in Jurassic World. For me...I want to keep doing these events not just for the Orbit but also to bring people into Wellington. There's always a problem...I read about Birmingham running out of funding which is a bit of a shame, and I think that funding is one of these great things that can help to bring people out. Whatever events we have organised have been free, and we work in the summer with the town council to bring people in. There are many events that people can't afford to go to, and at our events, they can attend for free and then have a wander around the town. If we had taken over the Clifton, we might have struggled because it was a bit out of the way, and you went there for a specific reason. The Orbit is in the square, and we can organise events right outside. People can come to our cinema, meet friends, pick up leaflets, and ask questions".*

Ray: *"And we are two minutes from the station!"*

Damian: *"That's right, people can come here from anywhere in the world, and we have free car parking...what more do you want? I was telling the Mayor Councillor the other day, "Please don't start charging for parking". In some other towns, they have put the parking prices up and increased the hours to eight o'clock at night, and people aren't happy. The other thing is that we haven't got enough parking spaces, and the car parks are getting full as Wellington's popularity grows".*

What do you like about being a projectionist at the Orbit?

"I have worked in theatre and in cinemas for most of my life and I have settled down here in Wellington. These days with streaming and everything else, to come out into a public space and watch a big screen with proper sound and watch a film

like that…you can't ask for anything more. It also encourages people to talk to each other which is important as we seem to be losing the enjoyment in good conversation and reading and watching and things like that. As a projectionist, I love choosing films; we have a wide range from arthouse to mainstream…some films are more successful for us than others, and some we bring back again and again. We have people coming from Wolverhampton, Shrewsbury, Stafford, Oswestry, we have even had two people from Cornwall because we were the only cinema showing Helen Mirren in "Parallel Lives".

Ray: *"We are more than a cinema, and we have boosted the economy!"*

What about your plans for the future of the Orbit and the town of Wellington?

Ray: *"Hopefully, by the end of next year, we will have finished the refurbishment of the upper floors, so we will have two performing studios, we will have an exhibition area and café overspill, we'll have some workshops and studios, we'll have meeting rooms for short term lets for people who want to do training or rehearsals or whatever, that will mean that we effectively maximise our utilisation of the building, because at the moment we are paying for the whole of the building and only using a third of it. That, in turn, will generate further profits for us, which will make us financially secure, particularly as we own the building and have no mortgage to* pay. Hopefully, that will generate a sufficient amount of cash reserves for a rainy day. But for anything wider than that, we will look to the wider artistic benefits of the borough really and we are hoping that they are granters. So, in terms of what we are doing, and I think it's our selling point, that we are not asking for a grant we are asking for a contribution towards an investment for the future".

An upward spiral!

Ray: *"Yes, exactly!"*

Damian: *"I agree!"*

Damian: *"When we have everything up and running, I would like to see us as the gateway to Wellington! People can come to us and find out what's going on and where to go for different things in the town. In doing so, to help Wellington grow and get bigger and better".*

Ray: *"At the moment, the population of Wellington is about 26,000, and it is projected to increase to thirty-one thousand. 31,000. If you look at our immediate catchment area, it is about 50,000 bit; we do serve the whole borough. I think the thing for Wellington is you've got to look forward; you can't use the past as a recipe for the future. Wellington needs to reinvent itself under its own terms, and by no means can it be a clone or a lesser clone of Telford Shopping Centre, so it will be small independent stores, leisure facilities, and that sort of thing that will attract people into Wellington. When you think about when I moved to Wellington in 1958, the population was about 12,000, and these days, Wellington has never been bigger, and Telford Town Centre has never been smaller. We have the infrastructure here to develop the place and develop it on its own terms, and I am sure that we will flourish on that basis".*

Chapter Thirteen

Wellington Angling

What is your name and the name of your business?

"My name is Mark Summers, and I own Wellington Angling. We sell everything an angler needs, including carp tackle, course tackle, baits, and accessories. If possible, we would like to be the main fishing supply business in Telford one day".

What is the most popular thing that your customers are looking for?

"That would be terminal tackle and hooks: These are important aspects of angling as they are the aspects that come into contact with the fish. Hooks come in various shapes, sizes, colours, and designs. They can be made from high-carbonized steel, stainless steel, or steel alloyed with Vanadium. Hooks are paired with lures or bait to catch fish, and they remain on the line during reeling. Some hooks are even designed for optimal performance. If you want to control the sinking speed of your hook and lure, weights and sinkers come into play. Additionally, they add extra weight to enhance casting distance. These items vary in shape and size, ranging from small one-gram weights to larger than five-ounce sinkers. Materials like tungsten, lead, tin, and eco-friendly alternatives are used to create weights and sinkers these days".

"There are also floats, bobbers, and indicators they all serve the purpose of floating in the water. They can hover over the bait or remain attached to the fishing line. When a fish bites, the float may be pulled underwater. These items help anglers gauge the exact location of the lure beneath the water surface. They are crafted from buoyant materials to achieve their main objective".

Why do people enjoy angling so much?

"Relaxation! It's a great way to unwind and get away from the pressures of modern life. There's a hell of a lot of water in Shropshire, and it's a great place to be an angler. we get a lot of repeat customers coming to see us. It's about catching a bigger fish each time and trying to beat your personal best. There's the River Severn that goes right through the county and through Ironbridge. There are also lots of pools where you can go angling, and they are run by the Telford Angling Association".

Are there any fishing stories that customers tell you when they come in?

"Fisherman's Tales...that's the main one; there is always someone who has caught one that's bigger than anyone else's! There are thousands of anglers in Shropshire, and we concentrate on carp and course fishing. Carp are intelligent and elusive, so anglers need to use strategy and skill. They come in different sizes, and there is always a chance that you might land a massive specimen. Fishing for carp often takes place in beautiful natural settings, and there is a strong sense of camaraderie among enthusiasts. Success in carp fishing requires dedication and perseverance and each outing brings the excitement of unpredictability and discovery. There are more people interested in fishing than ever at the moment...it might have to do with the pandemic and wanting to be in the fresh air again and be with people. There is also respect for the fish...it's catch and release".

How about night fishing? Is it still a popular pastime?

"Yes, it's still very popular. Night fishing for carp can be quite atmospheric when it gets dark, the water can feel quite mysterious, and carp come out to play. Imagine feeling a big carp tugging on your line under the stars or with just a small light to guide you. Carp are more active and feed more readily during low light conditions such as dawn, dusk, and nighttime, while they tend to be more cautious and less active during the daytime, seeking sheltered areas".

What kind of customers do you get?

"Everyone who comes here seems to know what they want, and if they bring their children, they know what they want to buy. Anyone who is a new beginner usually starts off basic with pole fishing, like I did when I was younger. They can then progress onto rods if they are enjoying it and take it from there. One of our lads has begun fishing, and we have started him off in the same way. He has moved onto rods now".

How long do fishing sessions last?

"When we go to France, I fish out for a whole week...a solid week! You can also enter competitions with huge cash prizes, such as "FishOmania," where I think you can win £100,000!"

Lastly, I believe that Hollywood actor Brad Pitt is a keen angler...has he ever been in?

"Yes, he's just over there buying environmentally friendly products on my wife's stall!" (Laughter)

Chapter Fourteen

Wellington Cycle Delivery

There was once a councillor in town

Who rode his bike round and round

Like the Pony Express

Without any distress

On a bike that was mechanically sound.

Can you let me know your name and role or roles in Wellington?

"I'm Councillor Anthony Lowe, and I represent the Shawburch Ward on Wellington Town Council. I am also a Liberal Democrat and the Liberal Democrats' Parliamentary Candidate for the General Election".

I wish you the best with all those things. I understand you are part of the delivery service that has started in Wellington. What is it called, and how did it start?

"It's called the Wellington Cycle Delivery Scheme WCDS for short, it started as a pilot project about eighteen months ago with the loan of a Cargo Bike from Shropshire Cycle Hub, which is based in Shrewsbury and a small group of group of volunteers, and we set about doing deliveries on behalf of people who are perhaps housebound, or they can get out but struggle to carry their shopping home. We decided that we would focus on small traders both within the market and in the area, so it would be good for Wellington traders, it would be good for people who need deliveries, and it would keep us volunteers fit! And of course, the other plus point is that it saves the planet because those last mile deliveries in diesel polluting vehicles are reduced".

"The pilot went very well…perhaps better than expected, and very quickly, we had ten volunteers, and we had started with four, and then the Cargo Bike that was on loan was reclaimed by its owner, so myself and a couple of other volunteers put a

project together to Wellington Town Council that they buy us a Cargo Bike which they duly did. It was a big decision, because it cost six thousand pounds, but that bike now is working very hard and it's out every market day from 10:00 am until 2:00 pm or 3:00 pm and we now have fourteen volunteers of whom two are ladies and twelve are men. We used to have a nickname…we used to call ourselves "The Boy Band", but now we have two ladies; we can't call ourselves that anymore! And we have a real sense of "Esprit de Corps" and "Bon Ami" and we all get on well together. We have a "WhatsApp group" I'm the rota manager, so I sort all the shifts out on a Saturday particularly, and the way it works is if someone is in need of a delivery, they ring a number or, better still, text a number, because we can't answer the phone when we're cycling and say, "Will you please collect a box of veg from Top Fruits" for example and we then go to Top Fruits and pick up a box and deliver it to the house in question, anywhere within a three-mile radius of central Wellington. We also collect items for charity shops, so we will go to people's houses if they are clearing out their houses or their attic, collect everything they don't want and take it to the charity shop of their choosing. We are here to support all the small traders with no fear or favour…we're not here to support Morrisons or Aldi or any of the other big shops; we are here to help the small traders".

That sounds fantastic…who had the original idea for this? Am I right in thinking it was someone from South Africa?

"Yes, there's a chap by the name of David Staniforth who was already volunteering at the Shropshire Cycle Hub at the Riverside in Shrewsbury, where we operated. I'm also a trustee of the Shropshire Cycle Hub. I wasn't then, but I am now. Yes, David Staniforth borrowed the Cargo Bike and thought, "I can make use of that in Wellington", so he pedalled it over here, and we got up and running. We also have a rickshaw, so if anyone wants a rickshaw ride, we can arrange that! We can take you and your shopping on the rickshaw or you and your husband on the rickshaw! But it is by arrangement because we typically use the Cargo Bike and will make special arrangements to use the rickshaw if required".

There's a business opportunity there for a romantic rickshaw ride to see the sunset over the Wrekin! When did the idea of a delivery service start?

"It started in November 2022, and we started by delivering the Christmas Cake Kits on behalf of Kelli at the Little Green Pantry, so we must have delivered over a hundred Christmas cake kits, and that's when we realised that we could extend this model. As you rightly say, David Staniforth and another chap called Kevin Kavinorkus and I got involved early on as well, and throughout the winter, rain or shine, the only thing that stops us is ice and snow! But apart from that, we have the

weather gear, and we are robust cyclists, and the Pony Express carries on!"

Have you ever had any funny experiences while delivering items on your bikes?

"So, I had a delivery of meat for "Anthony's of Wellington", and I took it to Shawbirch. I struggled somewhat to find the house and then when I found it, there was no reply. So, I hung the meat on the doorknob, and you can probably guess the rest of this story (laughter). On Monday, Anthony Nicholls received a call asking, "Where's my meet?" And I had hung it on the wrong doorknob! So, obviously, I had to reimburse Anthony, and he had to apologise profusely to his customer and the house where I delivered it; when they came back after a two-week holiday, there was some rather rotten meat hanging on their doorknob".

And you left a note saying, "We'll meat again!" Sorry, I couldn't resist that one!

"Very funny".

Okay, let's get technical. Can you tell me about the bikes? Do you all love your bikes?

"Yes, we do…some of us don't have e-bikes, but most of us do. We are all proficient cyclists, and we all have driving licences, which is a requirement. We are looking for volunteers, so if anyone listens to this or reads this, they are welcome to volunteer. The actual bike we've got is a TERN GSD, which stands for Get Stuff

Done! It's a long-tailed Cargo Bike, so we can get a couple of bags of potatoes on the back if we need to, and meat delivery, says, on the front, so it's got a good payload…a hundred-kilo payload. It's got a double-size battery, so it has a double-size battery life, but you are right. We do have bikes that we use ourselves when the TERN is in for its service. I also want to mention that the TERN has a nickname…we call it "Dolly" I don't remember why that is, but we do!"

Is there a minimum amount that customers need to order before they can have a delivery?

"No there isn't, we don't go out of the three-mile area, and we have had the odd delivery out in Muxton, and we have done longer deliveries in exceptional circumstances and there is no minimum charge. Typically, the customer would pay the retailer on the phone using a debit card. We don't really want to handle money, but we occasionally do where a particular reliable customer wants to always pay in cash. When we do on those occasions, we always have the correct change in a plastic bag".

So, it's free of charge and no fees are involved?

"Yes, that's right, it's completely free, and there is no charge. We will accept donations if someone wants to, which goes towards the maintenance of the bike, and we have had to buy a few items such as high-vis jackets, for example, and marketing material, of course. We run the service, as I have

said, from 10:00 am to 2:00 pm on Tuesdays, Thursdays, and Fridays and 10:00 am to midday on Saturdays".

How do you think that this service has contributed to the revival of Wellington since you started?

"Well, there is the recognition factor in that everyone can see we are out and about and people like that we are doing something for the town. As we get more eco-minded e-bikes are on the up, and the beauty about batteries is that no one has to feel sorry for us now when we are going up Hampton Hill, which is quite steep, as we can just put the bike into "Turbo" and get up there with a sack of potatoes on the back no problem. So, we were ticking a lot of boxes, really, and I suppose that it gives a sense of focus for the town and ties that in with what "Love Wellington" is doing and the way in which Wellington is taking off again as a destination town at last. We're not just charity shops and empty shops anymore…Wellington has come along a long way and has further to go!"

When do you think that Wellington's reemergence began?

"I think it probably started when Sally Themans was taken on by the Wellington Council. She is the idea behind "Love Wellington," and before that, she was involved with "Love Bridgnorth," which was a great success. She was taken on in about 2018, and she was able to recruit a lady called Paola Armstrong, who joined the payroll of the town council, and the

two of them became a dynamic duo. It goes back to 2019, about the time I was taken on as Mayor, actually".

Can you tell me about your time as the Mayor of Wellington?

"First of all, it was an enormous honour to be the Mayor of Wellington, and at that time, I was a Conservative; we are going to get party political here, and I ended up getting on the front page of the Shropshire Star because I "defected" was the word they used, to the Lib Dems after being a Conservative for many years…so that was a story. It was a great honour to be the Mayor, it's an apolitical role, and you do not put your politics first; you are there for everybody. I enjoyed that role very much. There was some ribbon cutting involved, and you have to engage with people in an open, frank, and pleasant way and listen to people and their problems and so forth. Then there are obligations that come with it, such as the Mayor's Civic Service in the Church once a year, the Mayor's Christmas Carol Service, and switching on the Christmas lights. There is also the Bayley Mile that takes place every May, where schools run in competition around the town, and in fact, this May, there will be an adult category as well. It was a pleasure to be the Mayor; normally, the period is twelve months, but I was asked to extend by four due to the pandemic. So, instead of finishing in May 2020, I carried on until September 2020 because the lady who took over from me was of a certain age and was isolating at the time. So, I did sixteen months as Mayor instead of twelve".

Can you tell me about the work that created the opportunity for change in Wellington?

"Well, there is a committee which is called the Wellington Regeneration Partnership, which consists of Borough Councillors, Town Councillors, and Officers of Wrekin Council. I have never sat on that committee, even as Mayor, but they have been instrumental in the regeneration of Wellington over the last four or five years. This partnership was behind the development of the Orbit Cinema and is now behind the conversion of the YMCA Building, which will become residential and retail below. Wellington has benefited from several grants, and even though the funds for Wellington Town Council are limited, they cover several amenities, and I was able to get solar panels fitted to the toilets by the bus shelter and reduce their electricity bill".

How do you see things developing in the future?

"Readers will notice that Market Street has become mixed-use, in other words, pedestrians and vehicles and a similar scheme is planned for church street, which would be from Vineyard Road past Station Approach to the corner on Market Street. So, that's all part of the traffic calming for Wellington; we need to discourage vehicles from going that way if at all possible, and because there are so many pedestrians, people with prams, and wheelchairs and so forth, it's important that we reduce the traffic. But for traders and those with mobility issues, it's important to keep it open for vehicles. Also, there

will be effectively a new square created outside the former YMCA because once that building is refurbished and the "Planning for Beauty" building nearby is rebuilt, that becomes a whole new retail centre. We also have community champions, one group who are litter picking and the other who become champions of their area in terms of reporting any incidents that are of concern, and of course, councillors like myself and we are responsible for our wards. So, anything that is going on Shawbirch, I want to know about it".

"One of the last things I would like to say is about the parking…one of the important things about Wellington is the free parking, so come to Wellington and don't go to Telford!"

*"Anyone who needs any deliveries, what we suggest is that you text the Wellington Delivery Scheme on **07398 136 120**"*

Chapter Fifteen
The Pheasant Pub

Two brothers run the Pheasant in town,

Like a comet, they never slow down.

Their hops fill the air,

In the old market square,

And everyone says, "It's their round!"

What are your names, and what is the name of your business:

Steve: *"My name is Steve Preston, and this is my brother Peter Preston".*

Steve: *"We are from the Rowton Brewery, Pheasant Inn, and the Wrekin Inn…all three, so three in one! The Brewery was started by our dad, Jim, about sixteen years ago, in 2008. Rowton is a small village about eight miles north of Wellington, so not too far away".*

Peter: *"It's famous for the Rowton Meteorite, which fell there in 1876, and we've named some of our beers after it…it's part of our history".*

Steve: *"We moved the business into Wellington seven years ago; we occupied the building at the back of the Pheasant to put the brewery in and took the Pheasant pub on".*

Peter: *"I think Dad's huge interest in beer production has had a lot to do with it".*

Steve: *"Dad has always been an advocate for real ale and has been in the brewing industry for 25 years with Hanby Brewery in Wem. He was a farmer throughout his life, and in 2001, he decided to rent the land out to another farmer and went to work for Hanby Ales. Then in 2008, he decided to start brewing ale on his own".*

Peter: "It's known as traditional Cask Ale!"

Steve: "*It's a really traditional real ale…it's what dad originally focussed on and what we focus on now. Traditional real ale is a cask-related product, and it's got no interference from being pumped full of C02 and any other means…it's a natural product. There is a local link because right across the road is where the Wrekin Brewery used to be, and they were the biggest brewery in Shropshire at the time until they closed years ago*".

What was going on when I met you the other day and there was all that steam surrounding like an inventor in a laboratory?

Steve: "*When you popped over, you caught us in a brewing day, so at that point in time, I was basically mashing it…which is basically mixing malted barley with hot water, which releases the natural sugars present and leads into the later brewing process*".

And how much Cask Ale do you produce?

Steve: "*In terms of what we produce…it's just under 7,000 pints a week!*"

Peter: "*What we are doing here has brought back the smell of beer to Market Street. It's the smell of the malt and the hops…it's from the steam that's produced during the process. You can smell it all the way down Market Street…the smell of beer brewing is back in Wellington*".

What would you say is your Unique Selling Point… your USP?

Peter: *"I would say it's that fact that we are family-led".*

Steve: *"We're proud to be an independent family business; it was started by our dad and further developed by us."*

How do you feel about how Wellington has developed in the last few years?

Peter: *"There was a time when there wasn't much going on, and there wasn't much investment and a lot of charity shops. Whereas now, you've got lots of independent shops, niche businesses, and a good amount of decent café's. There are also new ventures like the tapas place in the square and live music at places like the Wrekin Pub".*

Steve: *"Peter and I grew up in Wellington and went to school and college here, and how it is today compared to then is very different. The high street received investment in the form of cobbled streets, enhancing its appearance. However, despite this improvement, it still felt neglected and in need of further attention".*

Peter: *"There were some personal touches…there were the murals and that's about five years ago…that's what made it begin to feel better those personal touches".*

Steve: *"Things were pretty quiet for a while, but there are now more places for people to explore, and we have brought real ale back to the town. The first year we took this place on,* we won the CAMRA seasonal award. Since then, we have won the best pub in Telford and, in the last two years, the best pub in Shropshire!"

How did the pandemic affect you as a business?

Peter: "Well, obviously, the closure of the pub... but we kept the brewery going, and we were in touch with our customers. We were going around Wellington and Telford and dropping off beer, which kept us going. In terms of when we reopened, that was a very challenging time as we had to deal with a lot of regulations. It was a test...and I think we came out alright".

Steve: "The thing I am most proud of is that despite all that was going on, we didn't pour one drop of beer away. There were all these things on the news and big breweries with barrels of beer cascading down the drain, but due to the great customer base that we've got because we've got three pubs, and one of them is in Oakengates, they were really keen to support us and not throw any beer away, and we're very grateful for that".

What lessons to you think you learnt from this challenging experience?

"I think it was to stay close to our customers because, yes, we were delivering beer, but there were a lot of people living on their own during the pandemic, and we were able to chat with them during the home deliveries, which I think meant a lot... while keeping social distances, of course!"

Steve: *"One thing that the pandemic did was change the way people shopped. They didn't want to go into the big supermarkets; they wanted to be in the fresh air, go to local towns, and be with people, and it brought the whole town together. The lockdown also meant that people had more disposable income to spend and were happy to support local businesses".*

What kind of contribution do you think that "Love Wellington" has made to the town?

Peter: *"Sally and her assistant Paola from "Love Wellington" have done a fantastic job and successfully encouraged people to love the town and appreciate it. Their work also brought all the businesses together and created a great community spirit... it's really good- there is a great community spirit as a result".*

Steve: *"I think it's also worth mentioning Wrekin Town Council as well, as they did a lot of work in order to improve the situation and fill any empty shops by providing a grant to people who wanted to start businesses. The support of the Council was what made the other things possible".*

Peter: *"The money that the council put in really moved things along, and now there are lots more lovely shops. I think that Wellington will continue to get better and hopefully continue on the same path. There have been some collaborative events between businesses, and we all support each other, and it works well like that".*

Were you surprised by the success of the late-night market in Wellington?

Peter: "Fantastic, it did absolutely amazing, and why not? It's well supported by the community and has brought people from outside the town into the town".

How about your other pubs, are you organising things there?

Steve: *"At the Wrekin Pub, that's an events-led pub, and we have bingo, quizzes, open mike nights, and music".*

Peter: *"It's a grassroots thing about giving people the opportunity to for people, starting out to play their music and perform".*

Peter: *"Between these two pubs, you could say that this one brought traditional ale back to Wellington, and the Wrekin Pub down the road brought music back to Wellington.*

Steve: *We also have a pub in Oakengates called "The Fighting Cocks", which is real ale. This pub, "The Pheasant", has seven real ales and two special ciders, the "Wrekin Pub" has six real ales and one cider, and "The Fighting Cocks", the 9 real ales and 3 ciders".*

Peter: *"The thing am most proud of is that we have brought real ale and music back to Wellington with these two venues.*

Chapter Sixteen

Wellington H2A

Rob is a history man

whose murals cover a span,

Of makers who've lived

And crafted their gifts,

In good ole Wellington town!

Can you give me your name and the name of your organisation?

"I am Rob Francis, and I am chair of Wellington H2A, which is a community group that a couple of us started…myself and my friend Tony about fifteen years ago. That came from the idea that, at times, the town didn't seem to make the most of its public spaces. It's got that lovely square…not much room to fill and a good backdrop for music and other things. We thought that we could start putting on music in the square and the town council gave us the money to do that. Then we thought we could do some other things and we got drawn into it from there. We started to think about how the town could revive itself and how heritage and culture could be part of that…we are a tiny, tiny part of what's going on".

Would you say that you were there at the beginning of the revival of Wellington?

"It's hard to say when the beginning was as there have been groups who cared about Wellington. I think the Civil Society started in 1970. George Evans was around then and seeing what was happening to Wellington in that period…and as Telford grew, Wellington began to architecturally decline. There were also other people doing things, and about the turn of the century, about twenty years ago, there was a feeling that the town was in the doldrums. Me and Tony decided, "What are we going to do about that?" The vibe from some of

our friends was that they were giving up on it, and we thought that was a bit boring, so we thought we would do something".

You have an interest in history, could you expand on why that is?

"I have always found history intrinsically interesting; I studied history at university. Within the context of Wellington, there have been quite a few books written about the place, and there is the magazine "Wellingtonia", which continues to produce history articles. For me, history is all about using source material for doing cool stuff now. As someone who is a historian by background in Wellington, my interest is in how we use that stuff…how we can take nuggets from the town's history to bolster a sense of place, a sense of distinctiveness, because everywhere has a distinctive history to everywhere else. Within the context of being part of Telford especially, which is a new town and as Wellington was trying to regenerate itself in the last 15 or 20 years… it seemed that history was the best way to redefine the town and create a narrative that people could latch onto. With events such as the Summer Fayre, anyone can do that, but to do that on the date of the sanction of the charter in 1244 is a cool thing to do, and the fact that the procession is from 1773 gives it a rootedness and a rational for why you are doing it. So, for me, history is about narrative and a sense of place".

Your father was a respected figure in the town; what do you think his legacy is?

"My father, Ken Francis, bought his business in 1979, and it has now become Anthony's of Wellington after he retired a few years ago. The legacy of the town, I think, is that it was a kind of bridging business. A butcher's shop was very similar to what it would have been a hundred years ago, and it's also the kind of business that towns like ours are not rebuilding themselves on. Locally sourced, quality, all that kind of stuff, which I think bridges old Wellington and new Wellington. He managed to continue surviving and thriving while other businesses were falling away, taking retirement due to lack of footfall. So about 10 or 15 years ago, when the town didn't have such a good reputation, people would tell you that there wasn't much to go to Wellington for, but they would go to his shop. Therefore, I think he became a linchpin business, and when I was thinking about printing leaflets, posters and adverts for Wellington 10 or more years ago, it was things like his business that drew you into the town. I think his legacy is that he kept things going when things were perhaps falling away. The legacy for me is that this was my way into the town; growing up here, I was probably more involved than my friends were. I would work in his shop sometimes and get to know people and see how businesses in small towns become part of the fabric of the community. When it was raining, my father would lend a customer an umbrella, or if one of his elderly teachers who had dementia was looking lost over the road, he would take him to the barber's. I started to see how businesses are not just commercial entities in towns of this scale; they have become an integral part of the community".

"In other ways, he was the singing butcher and a member of a choir, and he did woodwork and all sorts of stuff. He made himself part of things, and I think Tony, who used to work for him and myself, saw that and sort of shaped how we were part of things as well. I am not being overblown about it, but it has become part of my identity. If you talk to my friends in London, they all know where I come from, and they all know where Wellington is; they can name Wellington characters; it's become part of my personality".

"Moving away does help you to see other places and I have only been involved with the town since I moved away. I sort of went to university, and I stayed away; perhaps if I had lived here, it might have been different…perhaps I have romanticised it a bit. I did see things in other places and thought, "Why does this work, and could it work in Wellington?" Like music for example, as a means for activating space and I think appreciating the things that we have. If you grow up in a small town, you spend a lot of time being grumpy about it, and then you move away and you realise what was great about it. Just today, I walked in from my mum's house, and it was a sunny day, and everyone was smiling at me, and the town was looking good, and there was a bustle about the place, and that's not the case where I live now. I think my work as an engagement specialist working with local government".

Do you think you have learnt anything from your role that you have been able to use when promoting Wellington?

"I really like the idea of citizen energy…people power, and what that can achieve. What we are seeing in Wellington is a mixture of old-fashioned council investment which is great and important, but I don't think that half as much could have been done unless people were ready to do something with it. There are lots of groups such as "Walkers Are Welcome", "Dot Hill Nature Reserve", and "Friends of Wellington Station"… Tony and me doing events. My work is about trying to bring people together in different ways, and I think what you saw in Wellington in previous generations was the public meeting format, with people sitting in rows and someone on the stage taking questions. How do we get past that? What's a modern version of that? Now it's things like the "Ideas Farm" we formed a few years ago, which gave birth to the "Clifton Group" and, ultimately, "The Orbit".

"That was more of a workshop format where you say, "How can we surface the energy in a place to make things happen? So, I guess what my work has helped me to do is to surface that energy to bring things together to make things happen. I think what you are seeing in Wellington now, especially with the newer businesses, is that they are getting together off their own bat, and they are not relying on the council to come up with a project. What you are seeing now in Wellington is that businesses have lit their own fires and have kept them burning".

Can you tell me about the Makers Dozen Mural Trail and how you developed it?

"The council had some funding a few years ago, and I had seen something online about France and how they used "Trompe-l'œil" which translates as "deceive the eye" in English. It's a way of painting on the sides of buildings and in blocked-up windows that creates illusions. In essence, it's what Wellington H2A is trying to do: use heritage as source material to do fun things and tell a story. It felt like a subtle way to bring colour into the town with art, and in a conservation area, there's on so much you can do with that. In some cases, we were able to put images exactly where they should be and provide relevance or at least use a building that was contemporary to the image. So, the mural on the side of Bell Street of the two Plimer brothers, who were sons of a clockmaker somewhere, probably in New Street, that's where the woodworkers were, and they ran away from home, we think and became famous artists in London. So, the idea of the mural trail is to tell the story of the town in another way and not just in a book. How can we bring history into the mind's eye and onto the streets...literally!"

And what about Charter Day? Was it before or after that?

"Wellington H2A used to do three things "Sounds in the Square", which was live music on a Saturday, "The Midsummer Fayre", which we have been doing in June and "Charter Day", which was supposed to be a simple thing to organise at a time of year when

there was nothing much going on. We realised that the charter was granted on the last day of February 1244 and tried to imagine how it happened and once again used history as a source of fun. Clearly, something would have to happen to inform the Lord of the Manor that he had been awarded a charter, so we would need someone to bring it on a horse. So, we imagined a King's rider on a horse brings it into the town square and reads it out. We aim to create opportunities for three pictures before, during, and after so that there is a sense of anticipation, of the event, and reporting on the event afterwards. "Charter Day" was a simple idea about celebrating the market charter...we've got this charter which is quite old and let's celebrate that! It was done to be free; the lovely lady brings the horse and does it for free, we have Morris Dancers which cost very little for what they do, costumes that are used for the "Summer Fayre" and businesses help out by taking part. We do it all for a couple of hundred pounds, and it's a spectacle for that time of the year...so that's what that is!"

The Market Square is a great place to try out ideas, don't you think?

"Yes, it's like a little amphitheatre, and H2A is all about using public space to create experiences. It's like today...it's quite sunny today, but there is nothing going on in the square, and it can feel quite empty, and all you need is a bit of music or something...I came through one day, and there were some ladies doing Tai Che, and I thought, "That's interesting!" it's just something visual. I have written about this before, in an *age where you don't need to go into your local town to buy anything when you can buy it online or at the supermarket, towns like ours need to offer something else. Therefore, it needs to be experiential and be somewhere you can meet your friends and have a coffee, have a beer, have lunch and see something or hear something. In this respect, the town didn't really do much of that historically; it didn't need to...and now it does. So, the square is a gift that is closed to traffic and a space where you can do things. While it was sad that saving the Clifton didn't for different reasons, it's great that you ended up with a cinema and soon-to-be arts centre right on the square that gives them a breakout space for things that they do. That's why we are keen in our little group about shop fronts and urban design because you want a space as small as Wellington to look as good as it can, and that square has a great big gap at the moment because the owner will not do it up or sell it, which is a great shame, and there are a few shops that haven't got great signage. That really is our showpiece space, and when you get off the train, you want to see that square sparkling. So, my ambition is that whilst the big projects at the market are being done and the YMCA Building that, we can also make that square sing as a public space!"*

What is the name of the building you are referring to?

"It was Stead and Simpsons...a 1930's building, I believe. If you look at it today from the market approach, it's in urgent need of repair. I know it would be expensive to repair, but I'm hopeful that we might be able to do something with it in the

future. To me, it's almost criminal that a prime space in the town is just being left to rot because of one landowner who doesn't want to repair it to sell it. I know there were some good businesses who wanted to move into that building and were not able to due to the cost of doing it up. I would like to see through planning or something a way to stop property owners from seeing buildings in this way as cash cows that can be left abandoned for long periods of time".*

Can you tell me about your involvement with the Midsummer Fair?

"When we first started doing sounds in the square in the summer, we did a folkie thing and invited some Morris Dancers to come along, and that was an attempt to rebrand Wellington as a place of history, which it had sort of lost. And by the way, people often blame Telford for that, but if you look at the 1950s and 1960s literature guides about Wellington at that time, there were a lot of business owners and property owners who also didn't care about history and were busy modernising. This was a major town for this part of the county, and there was very little concern for preserving it, and it wasn't really Telford's fault, so we were trying to increase the interest in the town's history and we were trying to present things that had been in books, in the street. So, we had one event, and then we thought…perhaps we have a historical fair. We went to look at the charter, and there was a June Fair sanctioned in the charter…a Summer Fair. Then we got the church involved because they've got the green space and were

respectful because it had been a cemetery. The church was very helpful and allowed traders to create a sort of village green feeling. We had music in the church, in the churchyard, on the green and in the square. So, the idea was to bring the town to life by using music and performance in order to show the population and businesses what the town can be when you activate it".

The Photographs of the Summer Fair look great, and you can see how much people enjoyed dressing up in historical costumes.

"When I was at university, I studied a lot of 18th-century history, and I'm a big fan of the period. The first year we did the Summer Fair, we got some lottery money, so we were able to buy some costumes, and some local ladies made some as well. The first procession was a bit of a fraud because a few of my work friends came from London and the procession was them! It probably looked quite scant, and people were probably wondering what we were doing. However, they have got used to it now, and it has become popular. It does look slightly ridiculous, but what me and Tony try to do is to inject some colour into the town. The murals are all about projecting colour into the town as well, and the processions are all about reimagining what the town must have looked like at some point. There is no high art to it, and it isn't deadly serious historical reenactment; it's simply using history as a source material for creating fun".

Are you working on any other projects at the moment?

"The main things with H2A are Charter Day and the Summer Fair; then, there are always things in the background, such as supporting good planning decisions and urban design. I'm not an urban design professional, but I have taught myself about architecture and design to help businesses think about how to present themselves and also talk to the council about that. I have recently written a guidance document about shopfront design, which I have worked on with Borough Council professionals which they linked and have used for new businesses or businesses that are re-branding. You might see a sign go up for a business that might not be great, and it might take the council a year or two to get it taken down and replaced. No one wants businesses to spend money unnecessarily. The town just degraded over time, and we are just trying to re-energise it and make it look the best that it can. That isn't always seen as a good idea and is seen as a luxury, but if you don't do that, then people might just stop coming, and you can't just open a shop and expect to start selling stuff. The town has to look as good as it can, so our events are about moments that do that. It's about trying to create an urban context within those things, and when I walk around the town, I want to feel good about myself. Because everyone, no matter where they live, deserves to feel good about where they live and have their spirits lifted. It's every business owner's responsibility for me to do their bit, and I try to help them".

How do you think that things are developing in Wellington?

"What interests me now as Wellington tries to re-forge its identity is the way in which, as Telford grew, Wellington didn't really know what it was anymore, and the town's role in the area was replaced by Telford. So, for me, history is a way in which it has been able to reform its identity. That doesn't mean looking backwards but being the source material for building your future from something distinctive, which is your past. I'm interested in how a high street can be inclusive, too, because history is everybody's, and Wellington is quite diverse by Shropshire standards. You have had migration to this area in the 19th and 20th centuries in different waves, and the way we weave that into the town's story is going to be important. One of the things I would love to do is to create a museum that provides a heritage space. This has been discussed before, and if you talk to councillors, you might find that they think it would be a bit tawdry and feature a mangle and an old copy of the Shropshire Star! For me, it's just a space again where everyone can tell their story and they can play their part. It's not so much as creating Wellington into a modern market town but getting the balance right and I think that Tony's business is a good example of that. There is always a risk of over-regenerating or over-gentrifying a town and leaving some businesses behind and you become a place where local people feel is not their place anymore. I don't think that there's a risk of that in Wellington because there is a really

good mixture of businesses. They sell at different price ranges, and you want a good mix. There are extensively some prettier market towns that people might visit as tourists in Shropshire and elsewhere. However, Wellington is in a healthier position because it's bigger, and towns need more footfall than they used to in order to survive. So, the fact that we have a lot of housing and well-priced housing compared to other places, and you see that reflected in the businesses as well where there are businesses run by other people now. The towns that are more touristy find it hard to survive out of season, whereas I think we have quite a sustainable town here now. There are lots of people moving in and lots of businesses with energy, and I think Wellington will be a template for what a market town can be".

What was it like for Wellington during the pandemic, and how did it cope?

"I wasn't living here during the pandemic; I was in London, so I couldn't get here. However, because of "Love Wellington" and the way it continued to keep everyone informed on social media, I was able to keep up with what was going on here. It contained lots of upbeat stories about how businesses were helping each other out and rallying around. At this lowest point, I guess everything was closed, but to segway into your other question, during that time, people who lived and worked in that doughnut around the town were confined to barracks, so to speak, and they were doing their walk every day and got to know the town better, perhaps love the town better, feel

more for it, willing it to do better. The timing is important because we're still seeing towns in this country struggling and high streets emptying out. Because of "Love Wellington" so you have "Love Wellington" telling the story in a positive way that hadn't happened on social media before, coupled with the town council putting its money into new businesses that would be about 2018/2019. So, the pandemic hit, that positivity was already there, and that carried through...had we been at the low point still in 2019/2020, then the pandemic might have been more of a negative story for us. I think we were in a good place going into it, and we saw out those years, and there was that pent-up energy commercial, socially, culturally, and when restrictions were lifted, and people want to visit the town again, all those things that were put in place before were really helpful".

Do you have any final comments about how the town could develop further?

"There has been some borough funding to help businesses take themselves online, and perhaps there is probably a very small amount of business where there isn't the support for the design element or online footprint that bigger businesses have. I am really positive about what is happening in Wellington now, but it's important that we don't take it for granted. There is an inherent fragility to anything around the high street at the moment. It's been doing well, even though there is a cost-of-living crisis and we haven't lost many businesses compared to other places, but you could imagine that any financial shop to the county for any sustained period and you could lose a lot of ground that we've gained quite quickly. I therefore think that collectively businesses and the town council continue to think about how they can make this situation even more solid. When H2A began to do things about 15 years ago, it was sometimes dispiriting, especially when you put a lot of energy into things, but we just wanted to keep things simmering and keep producing positive images of the town so that when things shifted, the town would be ready for it. So, like my father's business at that time and the other business, we were just keeping things moving and ready for what is now happening".

"I have always been an optimist, and vision is a grand word, but I had an idea of how I think Wellington could be and how it could work in the modern world that others didn't always see. What is reassuring is that we are seeing that in a way that is how I kind of imagined it would work, to be honest. It's about independent businesses, but not all high-end businesses; it's about events, but not all big events; it's about a jigsaw of stuff that is working quite nicely. What I would like to see now is more of the same now that we are on a trajectory which wasn't visible five years ago but now is. So, I think more of this...I think that the council's big investments through government funding in the market and the YMCA building are positive. I think what we need now is, with so many businesses wanting to set up here and lacking in good premises, we need to see investment in the physical buildings of the town to house the right businesses. There are several buildings that are on *pause, some bought by the council and in need of development and some by private individuals who are sitting on them. So, I think we need to see a continued effort to accommodate the businesses that want to set up here. I have to say that "Love Wellington" has been great, and all that investment and energy has been put into putting on a show so that throughout the year, there is always something happening that attracts people into the town. After years of trying to tell a good story about the town and being known back sometimes, I feel that the reality is now positive as well, and people are seeing that and buying into it. I think what is important is that it's regeneration that is owned by everybody! I think it's a good example of how government money and council money can't just do it on its own. It's got to land in a good place, and that's what we are seeing!"*

Chapter Seventeen

Anthony's of Wellington

Anthony's Butchers, a gem in the town,

With a farm shop and coffee that's ground

For quality bites,

And foodie delights,

It's the place where good taste wears the crown.

Can you let me know your name and the nature of your business

"My name is Anthony Nicholls, and the business is Anthony's of Wellington and Kinch's Coffee Bar and Bistro".

That is a combination of businesses; why have you decided to do that?

"My initial thought was just to incorporate the coffee shop and we thought that we would give the coffee shop its own identity and split the business up so that it made the business in a way more manageable. Kinch's is the maiden name of my mother, so I thought that I would name it after her for several reasons…she always wanted a shop, but my dad always said: "No, if you have a shop, you will give all your wares away and take pity on old ladies who want something cheaper, so no no no". Her money, inherited from her, has probably bought the shop she always wanted, and she loved coffee, and it was probably the only drink she drank as well as occasional red wine and barley wine…so it's Kinch's coffee bar".

How long have you been open for business?

"We are very close to our third anniversary in this shop, and previously I worked for Ken Francis, the butcher, who was about 50 metres up the road, and I started there in 1988 at the age of fourteen".

Looking back at old editions of "Love Wellington", I notice that you are in several editions and are one of the people promoting the town. Didn't you have something to do with the historical pictures in the doorways and windows?

"A few years ago, my boss Ken Francis and his eldest son Rob Francis graduated as a historian from Cambridge University and his idea was to bring the heritage of the local town alive because he grew up here as well and his father obviously owns a shop in the town. He formed a group called H2A (Heritage and Arts Alive), and we organised events; we were partly responsible for the ending stages of the Wrekin Barrel Race, where we hauled a barrel up to the top of the Wrekin in commemoration of the Wrekin Wakes where people would haul beer up to the top of the Wrekin and get a bit drunk. I had already begun to run my charity barbeque at Wellington Cricket Club, which ran from 2000 to 2010, and we raised money for the NSPCC and the Severn Hospice. That inspired Rob to form this group and do more events like that and keep heritage alive as well, so then he came up with Charter Day, which we have just had to commemorate the granting of the Wellington Market Charter in 1224 and the Midsummer Fair which brings a lot of stalls to the town…jesters street entertainers, and then we have a ceilidh and sometimes a barbeque in the evening and this year we are going to have a cold food spread. That links in with our French twinning town

of Chtenay-Malabry, and they all come over, and that's about 70 or 80 and at the Belmont Hall for that Shindig".

So, this all came before "Love Wellington" became involved?

"Obviously, love Wellington promotes massively anything good that's going on by social media, magazines, and word of mouth. Sally and Paola try to promote as many stallholders and shops as they can, and they also encourage businesses to work together. So, funnily enough, I took Pete from the Rowton Brewery opposite to one of their meetings last year, and he said, "That's great…let's do a collaboration" So Lee, my main man in the other room here is very keen on Barbeques and Grills, and he took them across the road to the Pheasant Pub which is also the home of the brewery, and we wheeled them over there and we filled the place, and we had an afternoon of barbeques and live music. There was a downpour before, a traditional British barbeque, and we all got soaked and then dried out from the barbeques, so all good in the end!"

Can you describe your role in the Charter?

"Certainly, I've done several roles in it, and you can be part of the court elite where you prove your worthiness to hold the keys to the market and the ale tasters, and the Mayor is there saying he will do his best for the town. Then Rob goes through a funny little script where he asks, "Are they worthy?" And we all say our piece, and we all say "Aye" obviously, and we all dress up in clothing from the Georgian era, although it would *have been from 1244 we some Georgian customers made via a grant and had them hand-made, most of them, funnily enough, made by a girl who used to work for Ken, and she made a beautiful golden gown which was worn by a chap from "Old Pals" in Market Walk. We have about thirty costumes, and we use those in the summer, and we mix and match some of those. We start off with Morris dancing from about 11:00 am, and then the King's messenger arrives on a horse and announces that the King has granted a market charter, and there is a mini celebration from the Morris Dancers to herald the way for the and the messenger and Rob has paraphrased the actual document that announces that the Charter has been granted. Then we do the court of officials and who will be taking which post, and then there is a bit of silliness where apparently if the court met, they would try the local villains, and we had Mr's Wysome, the retired teacher from New College who something of an eco-warrior and she as tried for ripping up someone's plastic grass and replacing it with real grass and she was acquitted!"*

Is she the wife of Bob Wysome, the music teacher who taught at New College?

"Yes…she is, and he sadly passed away several years ago, but he is immortalised on the boards mentioned, and Rob was able to get a grant to get historical characters painted on boards all around the town, and they all depict historical characters, and for where there is not a face for a historical character where we know they existed we have used people who are part

of the town past and present. So, my old boss Ken is here in the mural as you walk in, and so is Bob Wysome and the cheese lady from the market".

Why do you believe in Wellington so much?

"I grew up here, I went to school here, and funnily enough, I showed a friend my house last night because it's across the road from the Wrekin pub, and then we moved because my father was disabled and we need a place with a straight staircase and there was a butcher's near the new place called "Aston and Cole", so I was twelve and walking past every morning with my mother on the way to school and they said "He seems like a nice bright, happy chap…does he want a job?" So, I said "yes" and started there at twelve to fourteen, and if you're doing that, you feel part of the town, and you feel that you are useful for something and useful to the town, you are growing roots not just in your family, but in a shop which is frequented by people who are living in and around yourself and there are friendships and relationships built up from that. You are literally rooted in and invested in all those relationships. It gives you a historic feeling that you are carrying on an ancient trade, and you start off sweeping the floor and making tea and all of those things, and then you process to making sausages and begin to learn the trade. That business then split up and went their separate ways, and Mum came into town and approached Ken; she asked if he would give me some part-time work as I had experience, and he said "no" because he said he had had some part-timers and they

had been useless. However, my mother badgered him again, I think, and he said "yes," and that was that!"

"Because Ken was a lynchpin of the town and sang in the choir and later in Bob Wysome's choir, he was a soloist and member of the snooker team, billiards team, and dart's team. He was the life and soul of the town and one of the major players. He brought me up the same and took me to cattle markets, when I was older, we went drinking together, we played snooker together, we sang together. My dad passed away at nineteen, and he became something of a father figure and, again, a massive investment in the town, and he was, in my eyes, the main man. He was a kind of mentor; he taught me the guitar, he was president of the Telford and Wrekin Butcher's Association chain of office several times and organised their dinner dances, he was a very good golfer…a single figure golfer, and he was the main man!"

How did you start your own business?

"Ken's health was, unfortunately, suffering because he developed inflammatory rheumatoid arthritis, so he had to take a back seat, so that was ten years ago, roughly speaking, and then COVID-19 came along, and we were working really hard selling cheese for Lisa, the cheese lady and cakes for Gratitude café, and we were selling a bit of veg…just to keep the town going. The decision was made by the market company at the time to close the entire market, and I fought them on that and said, "Why don't you sell outside in the outside market...you can sell veg, and there are only seven food stalls...people need feeding there are people in their eighties and nineties queuing up in car park, metres from each other, to buy poorer quality food generally from the supermarket. The company were not particularly happy about that, and in the end, we were operating in a room smaller than the one we are in now; we made it work; we were sending food out to people, and we were working silly hours. Then around 2021, Ken decided that he would sell the business, and I bought the business from him, and then I had to deal with the same company because they owned his shop, and they were asking for an increase in the rent, and I said, "We have covid to deal with and I have six members of staff to support and there are only a few customers on the street and one minute I am busy and the next it goes quiet, so I said...can I buy the shop?" However, this was not possible, and I had the opportunity to buy this place due to an inheritance from my late mother, who had passed away recently. I knew that Bob, who owned the fishing tackle and the gun shop, was thinking of selling up; totally unsuitable, and we had some building to do, but luckily, I have some very good friends who lent me the money, no pieces of paper, no contract, and I was able to buy this shop, and it wouldn't exist without them! Now I am in the fortunate position where I will not have to pay rent for the rest of my life, but we had to do a lot to the building first. We built this place...lots of us! We had to dig a trench for the plumbing, and I borrowed a pneumatic drill from one of my friends, who is a builder and dug the trench myself with this chap called

Josh. I hand-built all that wooden section up there and designed how I wanted everything in my head and told the plumber, "I want this here and the sinks there"

The interior of Kinches café is presented in a tasteful contemporary style which could easily grace the cover of any lifestyle magazine or supplement. How was this achieved?

"The colour scheme came from a lady called Amanda Goode, who suggested that colour, or something similar and the paint came from Wilko's next door. Now she worked as an art and design teacher at Bristol University until recently, and she just popped her head in. I know she has been instrumental in the decorations at "The Old Orleton", which used to be "The Falcon". It was beautifully decorated, and when you walked in, it was not what you expected in Wellington…she lifted the game. She has just retired and has had years and years of experience, and she suggested these colours and the feature walls".

And the artistic sign on the wall…who painted that?

"This sign is painted by Andy Field. He's been on TV, and his work has been in a programme that starred the comedian John Vegas. His connection to me is that Andy was also the sign writer for Ken, and I saw how he just sat there and painted it there and then. You can order a sign that is printed, but this kind of sign writing is another ancient art".

When did you start to notice that the town was improving in some way?

"Because I have worked in the town from 1988, there are times when you feel that things are going in a better direction, and then something happens and whether it is COVID-19 or the three recessions that Ken worked through when I was there. Unfortunately, things have a stop-and-start nature, and some good businesses start when something bad happens. Yes, at the moment, we have investment coming in, and yes, things are improving, and we are fairly secure here... but you never know, and you have to keep that in mind if you are in business. We have Chris Evans developing that land on the old Clifton cinema site, and the pub across from me, "The Pheasant", is going from strength to strength, winning the pub of the year, etcetera, and we work with them in collaboration and enjoy doing that. I do feel that unless something else comes out of left field, like COVID-19 or a recession, for example, or even an election. I do feel that ourselves, The Pheasant, The Orange House have really raised the bar. The Boot Micro Pub has a lot of potential, but just as it opened, the council dug up the road for about seven months, which was three months more than they initially said, and the car park over the road shut for three months. That affected our business and the Boot, but they have since been able to re-open. We also have a Wetherspoons; some people do not like it - it's a different dynamic and demographic. However, their footfall is brilliant, and you can get fish and chips there at twenty to eleven at

night and a pint, and it is still quite vibrant, and they won't make any nonsense. They have decorated the premises with William Withering in mind who discovered digitalis and was born in the square".

"It's the council and "Love Wellington" that have given the businesses the means to be what they are. These aspects are most welcome, and events like Charter Day do attract people to the town, but things like "Love Wellington" can reach more people than we can even though we all have our own Facebook pages because there are so many businesses out there shouting "look at me" it really helps if you have that blanket coverage of businesses working together. We are in a position to use word of mouth in our business, and if we let them know that something exciting is happening, they will invariably tell their friends".

How would you like to see the town progress in terms of all the businesses?

"Burying the hatchet with whatever grievances they have because some do, which is natural. You are only going to gain more prosperity by working together and getting along, not just saying negative things to the council but using constructive criticism. I think I have got to the stage where I am listened to, but there is an election coming up!"

And ideally, if you were in charge, what would you do?

"I would listen to people who have lived and worked in this town for most of their lives, Peter Jones Carpets, for example, and when they re-jigged this road, they made several huge mistakes. We went to what they call a "consultation", and nothing was listened to, and people have tripped up, and they have also banned any loading...thirty-two businesses with no rear loading. How is that going to work? There are only two loading bays, and one of them blocks access to the market; they needed an ambulance and a fire truck, and they couldn't get in. Infrastructure...two islands here and there to increase the traffic flow. There are four other islands that work perfectly, and they have blocked up the traffic lights. So, at school time you have three schools and there is a gridlock...it's not too long, but long enough to put people off popping into town before or after the school run. If they can't stop here, they will go elsewhere, and we have lost an opportunity".

Can you describe some of your products:

"We will start with the pottery that we use, which is made at Wenlock Pottery; you can see all the little blue and red bird designs, and all the bowls we use are made there. Over here the coffee we use, we blind tested them, and we use "Iron and Fire" from Shrewsbury and Honduras is our favourite. Henstone distillery from Oswestry won the "International distillery of the year" last year with the Gin Guides Awards. They go from strength to strength and their "London Dry Gin"

won the spirit award in San Francisco 2021, and you can't argue with those accolades. It's a father and son, and I think that the daughter has been taken on as well, and they have just had a massive investment from a guy who owns a football club somewhere. They are fabulous people to work with, and they're great. We also use "Moonshine Fuggles" based in Ironbridge, so we have a lot of their spirits. There is also "Halfpenny Green", a family business again, and I do think that their wine is the best grown in this country. We also have Paso Primero, which is from Spain and grown in the Pyrenees, but the guy who makes it lives in Shrewsbury and he's called Tom, and he literally delivers it himself. I also have to mention that Will Macken is an artisan charcuterie from Shrewsbury. He is brilliant, and you won't get salami of that quality made from this side of Italy".

Do you go out and find your products, or do they find you?

"A bit of both, I sent Lee, my right-hand man here, to the Ludlow Food Festival, just as we were setting out really to see who we could work with and what products we want to put on the shelf. Two farmers crisps, Lee met them and had a chat, and at this event, you meet the actual person rather than a representative. Will and his sister work together, and they are very small and very niche, and they care about what they do, and those are the sort of products I want to bring here. Because the customers I want are the ones who care about what they are eating, what they are putting on their table, and what they are drinking. Tina Caulfield is a local photographer, and we sell her bits and pieces, and she produced the picture in our window. I think we have eleven beer brewers at the moment we have the Salopian Brewery, Hobsons' Wye Valley. There are some really nice products just out of the county but close enough to be included. In terms of cheese, we have the Shropshire Blue, but I am careful not to sell anything that overlaps with the Lisa, and we have Cheshire and a friend who does pop-ups in the summer under the name mouse-hole. My wine range comes from Addison's in Newport, so Sue Richardson came and did a presentation and suggested reds and whites and which rose wine would complement the food and she remembers being lost in the hustle and bustle of the market as was, and Ken my old boss traced her to where she might be and carried her back to where her mother was parked, and she still remembers that vividly, and I use her and her husband to source wines. They are a brilliant company…I can send an email for an order at 7:00 am in the morning, and it is here by five in the evening usually…you can't get that with most companies. We also have honey from a company called "From the Beehive" in Dawley, which is another great company. The birthplace of Captain Webb, so it's a historical place and like all the people we work with, they really care about what they do".

Do you have any vegetarian or vegan products?

"We have well-sourced vegetarian and vegan products as well as our meat products".

Do you have any *Flexitarian* customers who enjoy a mixture of all of them?

"Yes, you!" (laughter).

Gallery

Historic Wellington

Wellington rediscovered

A sign of the times

The Revival Begins

Working together

Time to celebrate

Up and running

Success!

By the same author.

A Prince rescues a woman who wants to be famous!

"I have read the book and it is clever, very well-written, and will help many readers."
Dr Jeffrey Zeig

HOW TO MANAGE RESCUER FEELINGS

In a Post-Pandemic World

DR TADZIO JODLOWSKI

A guide for rescuers everywhere!

Music:

Album

Stadium Soundchecks

by Tadzio*Presents

EP

Lights Down Stadium On

By Tadzio*Presents

Available on Bandcamp

Notes

Notes

Printed in Great Britain
by Amazon